AN ANGLICAN-METHODIST COVENANT

Common Statement of the Formal Conversations between the Methodist Church of Great Britain and the Church of England

ISBN: 978-0-7151-2246-4

Published 2001 by Methodist Publishing House and Church House Publishing.
PB140
GS 1409

© 2001 The Archbishops' Council and the Trustees for Methodist Church Purposes

All rights reserved. No part of this publication may be produced, stored in a retrieval system, transmitted, in any form or by any means, electronic, mechanical, photocopying, recording or otherwise, without the prior permission of the publishers Methodist Publishing House, 20 Ivatt Way, Peterborough PE3 7PG

Printed by Stanley L Hunt (Printers) Ltd, Rushden, Northants

CONTENTS

Foreword	v
Introduction: The Purpose and Scope of this Common Statement	1
Methodism and the Church of England	2
Our Churches Today	10
The Healing of Memories	14
Anglicans and Methodists Working Together	16
Fifty Years of Anglican-Methodist Conversations	19
The Formal Conversations	24
Sharing in God's Mission	27
Full Visible Unity	34
A common profession of faith	34
One baptism and one Eucharist	39
A common ministry of word and sacrament	44
A common ministry of oversight	54
An Anglican-Methodist Covenant	60
Recommendations to our Churches	62
Bibliography	63
Appendices	65
Index	70

FOREWORD BY THE CO-CHAIRMEN

It is with great pleasure that we commend the report of the Formal Conversations between the Methodist Church of Great Britain and the Church of England to our two churches and to ecumenical partners for a process of study and response. At the end of nearly three years of hard work and intense discussion we believe that we have carried out the task laid upon us by the General Synod of the Church of England and the Methodist Conference. We feel confident that the report and its joint declaration, if approved by our churches, will enable them to take a significant step forward together.

The method that we were mandated to follow is that of seeking greater visible unity by a series of agreed stages. Building on decades of Anglican-Methodist theological convergence and practical co-operation locally, regionally and nationally, our report makes possible the crucial step of mutual affirmation and mutual commitment. In doing this, the churches will be endorsing in a formal way what is already a reality in many local situations. We are convinced that that is a necessary and important thing to do.

Some will be disappointed that we have not gone further. However, the goal we were set was realistic and deliverable. It was not a high risk strategy. After the failure of the unity scheme in 1972 and the abortive Covenanting for Unity proposals of a decade later, a high risk strategy was not appropriate. We cannot afford to fail again. We need to proceed in a steady but resolute way towards our goal which is as ever the full visible unity of Christ's Church. We believe that the method of the Formal Conversations is one suited to our circumstances. But we see the Anglican-Methodist Covenant we propose as a stepping stone on the way to further developments in the near future. We believe our churches should implement the terms of the Covenant with all speed.

One of the distinctive features of the report is the way it develops the argument that commitment to mission and commitment to unity cannot be separated. The visible unity of the Body of Christ in the world, still to be realised, will be a fruit of the reconciling mission of God. We give special attention to the theology of mission to help enable the release of energy on many fronts. We pray that the further we travel together the more energy will be released for mission: shared evangelism, public witness and service.

A second striking feature of *An Anglican-Methodist Covenant* is the depth of the portrait of visible unity. We have followed the pattern endorsed by our churches in the preparatory report, *Commitment to Mission and Unity*, and have structured our work by expounding the characteristics of visible unity. We begin with confessing the apostolic faith together and work through the ministry of the word and sacrament to the forms of conciliarity and oversight. Our main focus has been on principles that are constitutive of the Church, not on particular structures. In this way, we trust that our work will be relevant to other ecumenical encounters.

Another important emphasis is the way we seek to bring out the reality of *koinonia* (communion, fellowship and participation in the life that the Spirit gives) in our churches. We have worked to discern in each other the authenticity of our life as churches. This discernment is articulated in the first part of the Joint Declaration, the Affirmations. We echo the language of the Reformation, with its quest for assurance about where salvation is to be found, when we solemnly acknowledge and affirm each other's churches as true churches (albeit imperfect ones) belonging to the one, holy, catholic and apostolic Church of Christ.

The language of Covenant is important. As we have already suggested, it picks up the many covenantal relationships at the local and regional level between Anglicans and Methodists, and indeed with other Christians too. It is also a profoundly biblical term. In Scripture, God's covenant with his people is made by grace. It involves forgiveness and healing. It survives the ups and downs of human nature and human experience, for it is God who calls and enables and God keeps faith. Our own proposed covenant involves a major commitment to work together, at every level of church life, in all the ways that now become appropriate and to strive to overcome the remaining obstacles to further and fuller forms of visible unity.

We would like to express our thanks to all the members of the Formal Conversations, including the ecumenical participants. We have very much valued their contributions. We are especially grateful to those whose unstinting hard work has brought the report to completion.

John B Taylor   **+Barry Rogerson**

INTRODUCTION: THE PURPOSE AND SCOPE OF THIS COMMON STATEMENT

1   This Common Statement proposes a new relationship between the Methodist Church of Great Britain and the Church of England. It culminates in a proposed Anglican-Methodist Covenant for England of mutual affirmation and mutual commitment, as a major stepping-stone towards organic unity. The provisions of this Covenant between our two churches are put forward for implementation with all due speed and rigour under the guidance of the Holy Spirit.

2   The Common Statement has several sections. First, it traces some of the ways in which Anglicans and Methodists have interacted in the history of the Church in England during the past two and a half centuries. The Statement builds on the Anglican-Methodist discussions of the 1960s and on the growth in fellowship since then in many areas of the churches' life, especially locally. It devotes substantial space to exploring the connection between unity and mission. It works steadily through crucial theological issues concerning unity in faith, ministry and oversight. Space does not allow a detailed rehearsal of all the study and discussion that the Formal Conversations have undertaken in these areas. The report does not pretend that all of these issues have been resolved, but it is clear that there is sufficient agreement for the two churches to take the next step that was envisaged when the Formal Conversations were set up. The Conversations believe that they have fulfilled the task that was entrusted to them and hope their work will pave the way for the next stage of unity between Methodists and Anglicans in England.

3   The Formal Conversations were set up by the Church of England and the Methodist Church of Great Britain in 1997-98. This was the latest step in a relationship that had had its ups and downs for two and a half centuries. The task of the Formal Conversations was to seek to draw up an agreement, in the form of a Common Statement, including a Declaration of affirmations and commitments. If endorsed by the Methodist Conference and the Church of England's General Synod, this agreement will bring the two churches into a new relationship at every level.

METHODISM AND THE CHURCH OF ENGLAND

Perceptions and realities

4 Because at its beginning Methodism was a movement within the Church of England it seems strange to ask whether the church which is most directly a descendant of that movement is able to agree a common statement of faith with the Church of England. John Wesley was a high churchman as the eighteenth century understood that term. So in 1745 at the time of Bonnie Prince Charlie's invasion Wesley was suspected of Jacobite sympathies, that is to say, of wishing to restore the House of Stuart to the throne. Methodists were never expelled from the Church of England unlike those who were deliberately 'dissenters' or 'nonconformists'. Nevertheless even in Wesley's lifetime, and certainly from his death in 1791, Methodism grew apart from the Church of England. More than anything else it is the simple fact of separate development which means that the two churches find certain things strange about each other.

5 Both churches have also tended to tell their own story in terms of myths about each other. It is often said that the 18th-century Church of England was moribund, that it was unwilling and unable to respond to the spiritual needs of a growing population. In such a scenario the Evangelical Revival in general, and Methodism in particular, brought the gospel to a population otherwise deprived. Similarly it is suggested that the Church of England only recovered a true sense of its pastoral vocation and its nature as a church as a result of the Oxford Movement between 1833 and 1845. This led to a renewed sense of the seriousness of schism within the Church, and a repudiation of the protestant character of the Church of England.

6 These historical stereotypes have recently been challenged. The 18th-century Church of England was not as moribund as has been supposed – indeed some bishops were conscientious in travelling great distances in an age before transport was easy. The history of Methodism was not a smooth progression with steadily increasing evangelical success. The levels of church attendance in the 19th century indicate the relative failure of the Evangelical Revival as much

as its success. The extent and significance of the high church tradition in the Church of England before the Oxford Movement was seriously underestimated by John Henry Newman, who came from an Evangelical background.

7. Furthermore, the pastoral revival in the Church of England sharpened the division between church and chapel. In the 1790s the Anglican theologian, William Paley, as Rector of Bishop-Wearmouth, attended the Methodist chapel in his parish from time to time, and encouraged its work, even though he disagreed with its theology, because in a large urban parish with insufficient Anglican resources he felt it was doing good among the poor. Half a century later there had been an increase in the number of Anglican clergy and a significant church-building programme; legislation against clergy holding livings in plurality and against non-residence in the parish. That meant that the clergy, particularly in villages, were more likely to see nonconformists as rivals rather than potential allies; and that feeling was returned, even though many people still identified themselves as 'church *and* chapel'. By the end of the 19th century, Anglicans and Methodists seemed to be inhabiting different worlds.

John Wesley's Methodism

8. John Wesley (1703-91) was born in Epworth, Lincolnshire, the 13th (or 14th) child and second son of a Church of England clergyman, who had a dissenting upbringing, and whose wife was the daughter of a distinguished dissenting minister. His upbringing and his time as an undergraduate at Christ Church, Oxford were deeply influenced by the conscientious spirituality of the Anglican non-jurors. (They declined to take the oath of allegiance to William III, and consequently had to resign their offices.) One significant influence was William Law's *Serious Call to a Devout and Holy Life*. Another influence was that of the religious societies which developed at the end of the 17th century, particularly in London. Although these were within the established Church, the common discipline of their members was very similar to that of dissenting congregations. The 'Holy Club' at Oxford, in which Wesley was involved with his younger brother Charles (1707-88), met regularly for prayer and Bible study, and this was to become characteristic of the subsequent Methodist classes.

9. The name 'Methodist' had overtones of earlier controversies, but was first applied to the Wesley brothers in 1732 and subsequently to George Whitefield. It seems to have been used, in part, because of their rigorous rule of life. In the early years the Evangelical Revival brought together people of widely differing opinions. The Wesley

brothers' time in America from 1735 to 1738 brought them into contact with the Moravians, and thus with European Pietism and the network of those interested in revival on both sides of the Atlantic. After John's 'conversion' experience in Aldersgate Street in 1738, he followed the example set by George Whitefield (1714-70), acknowledged by contemporaries as the leader of the Evangelical Revival in England, by preaching in the open air. The term 'Methodist' was also used of the independent revival movement in Wales, led by Daniel Rowland and Howell Harris, which led to the formation of the Calvinistic Methodists (now the Presbyterian Church of Wales).

10 As Wesley gathered preachers around him – some ordained within the Church of England, others not – he began a series of annual conferences with them in 1744. At the first meeting, they defined their aim as 'to reform the nation, more particularly the Church; to spread scriptural holiness over the land'. Wesley's preachers formed societies in the places where they preached, though members were always encouraged to attend their parish church, and Methodist services were held at a different time. The societies formed a 'Connexion', similar to other products of the Revival – the New Connexion of General Baptists, for example, or the Countess of Huntingdon's Connexion which gathered churches under the Calvinist influence of Whitefield and was even more insistent on the use of the Anglican liturgy than those associated with Wesley.

11 The difference between Wesley and Whitefield over Calvinism (see paragraphs 112-120) had become apparent as early as 1741, though Whitefield was usually conciliatory. Most leaders in the Evangelical Revival took a Calvinist position in the 18th century, albeit a 'moderate' one, and this was true within the Church of England as well as without. After Whitefield's death in 1770, antagonism became more marked. From 1763 Wesley's *Notes on the New Testament* and the four volumes of his sermons had been incorporated in the model trust deed for Methodist buildings; they are still the secondary doctrinal standards of the Methodist Church today (see paragraph 107).

12 The situation was complicated by Wesley's concern for his American societies after the Declaration of Independence in 1776. The Church of England's unwillingness to ordain bishops for America led him in 1784 (though a presbyter) to ordain two men deacon and presbyter and also to ordain Thomas Coke (already a presbyter in the Church of England) as a Superintendent for the oversight of Methodists in America. Wesley instructed Coke to

ordain Francis Asbury as his colleague in this episcopal ministry. In the same year Wesley made legal provision for a group within the Methodist Conference (the Legal Hundred) to exercise oversight of the movement in perpetuity. Although Wesley remained a presbyter of the Church of England until his death, it became increasingly difficult to maintain that John Wesley's Methodism was part of the Church of England.

After Wesley

13 The tensions which Wesley had kept in check during his lifetime exploded after 1791. Particularly in the towns, chapels wanted to hold their services at the same time as those in the parish church; this was quickly allowed. Travelling preachers were also allowed to administer baptism and Holy Communion in Methodist chapels, if a majority in the local society so wished. But the lay leaders in many places resented their exclusion from any voice in the policy of the Connexion. The result was a separation of a number of Methodists in 1797 to form the Methodist New Connexion, with equal lay and ministerial representation in the Conference. The other development was the imitation of American revival methods in the form of camp meetings after 1800. Notwithstanding Wesley's long journeys on horseback, revival meetings of the kind which became normal in America were generally absent from England. When these mass meetings began in the early 1800s, involving several hundred people at a time when there was no police force and the government feared the example of the French Revolution, the Wesleyan leadership banned them, and affirmed their loyalty to the Crown. The result was that revivalist movements developed separately.

14 The Primitive Methodist Connexion was founded by Hugh Bourne and William Clowes, both of whom were expelled by the Wesleyans because of their participation in camp meetings. Although class tickets were first issued in 1811, the first Conference (with two representatives to every preacher) took place in 1820. By 1851 Primitive Methodist membership had reached more than 100,000. The Bible Christians were formed by William O'Bryan in 1816; their first Conference was held in 1819. Both the Primitive Methodists and Bible Christians had women itinerant preachers at first. What has been called 'a second harvest of revival' was reaped in areas like Lincolnshire, the East Riding of Yorkshire, East Anglia and the South West from the 1820s. In these traditions there was little attempt to follow the Prayer Book pattern of worship.

15 Nevertheless, Wesleyan Methodism continued to grow rapidly in the early 19th century, more than trebling in size between 1801 and 1841, when there were well over 300,000 members. In 1836 its Conference decided to ordain itinerant preachers with the laying on of hands. Coming, as it did, hard on the heels of the founding of the first Methodist Theological Institution for the training of itinerant preachers, this seemed to accentuate the difference between them and the local preachers, upon whom most of the preaching in Methodist chapels still depended. The question of the nature of the pastoral office was close to the heart of the divisions in the second quarter of the century, which produced the Wesleyan Methodist Association in 1836 and the Wesleyan Reform movement in 1849. (The latter division arrested Wesleyan growth for a generation.) Thus, ironically and possibly unhelpfully, disagreements over the nature of the ministry were articulated in terms of the place of the laity in church government. It was only after the Wesleyan Conference agreed to admit lay members in 1878 that reunion with the other Methodist traditions became possible.

16 The Wesleyan Methodist Association and the majority of Wesleyan Reformers formed the United Methodist Free Churches in 1857. In the early 20th century they, together with the Bible Christians and the Methodist New Connexion, united to form the United Methodist Church (1907). Discussions began after the First World War between the United Methodist Church, the Primitive Methodist Church and the Wesleyan Methodist Church which led to the formation of the Methodist Church of Great Britain in 1932.

Changes in the Church of England

17 The Church of England was changing too. Many Anglican Evangelicals, whose influence was growing in the age of Charles Simeon (1759-1836), did not like Methodist intrusions into their parishes, and in any case tended to be on the Calvinist side of the theological spectrum of that time. But the Oxford Movement of the 1830s heightened interest in the catholic traditions of the Church of England, with a new emphasis on episcopal succession as the test of catholicity. Fears that this led inevitably in the direction of Rome were accentuated by the move of leading figures such as John Henry Newman, Henry Manning and Robert Wilberforce into the Roman Catholic Church in the 1840s and 1850s. In fact, the majority of those influenced by the Oxford Movement remained within the Church of England, led by John Keble and E. B. Pusey. By the end of the 19th century the views of Anglo-Catholics could no longer be ignored, and

the work of such priests in many slum parishes (sometimes because it was difficult to find others to work there) had established a significant new tradition in Anglican worship and theology.

18 For those in this tradition nonconformists were at best schismatics and at worst heretics. There was certainly no case for recognising their ministers as ministers of word and sacrament or their churches as part of the catholic Church. Nor was any distinction drawn between Methodists and other nonconformists. The influence of Anglo-Catholicism on nonconformist perceptions of the Church of England should not be underestimated. In the 1840s the fear of 'popery' in the Church of England led even the most conservative Wesleyans to ally with nonconformists almost for the first time. The Evangelical Alliance was one manifestation of this. Some more radical Wesleyans and other Methodists were drawn to support the Anti-State Church Association and to criticise the principle of establishment. These national developments, set alongside an increasing sense of competition between different churches in the towns and villages of England, made the situation in the mid-19th century significantly different from that in previous centuries. The Lambeth Conference of 1888 sought to remedy this by adopting, as a basis for 'home reunion' (i.e. in the English-speaking world), the four points agreed on by the American bishops at Chicago in 1886. These were the Scriptures, the Apostles' and Nicene creeds, the two dominical sacraments of baptism and the Lord's Supper, and the 'historic episcopate'. Although this last phrase was carefully chosen to include a variety of interpretations (a point sometimes overlooked), it nevertheless put a question about the validity of non-episcopal ministries which proved easier to pose than to resolve.

19 Another manifestation of high church influence was the movement to restore the instruments of the Church of England's self-government, the Convocations of Canterbury and York, which began to meet regularly again from the 1850s. In 1886 Archbishop Benson established a House of Laity to meet unofficially with the Canterbury Convocation, and this happened in the Province of York in 1890. The difficulties in getting ecclesiastical legislation through Parliament led some Anglicans to argue that the Church should be able to legislate for itself without parliamentary involvement. The Scottish Episcopal Church (which was not established) and the Church of Ireland (which was disestablished in 1869) offered alternative models of self-government. The disestablishment campaign in Wales (which led to the inauguration of the Church in Wales in 1920) ensured that this issue remained on the ecclesiastical as well as the political agenda.

20 In 1903 the two Convocations and Houses of Laity began to meet as the Representative Church Council, and in 1919 the 'Enabling Act' made it possible for a reconstituted Church Assembly to pass ecclesiastical measures which, if approved by both Houses of Parliament, would have the force of law. For the first time since the Reformation this raised the question of whether the Church of England was a distinct body within the nation, as opposed to the nation in its religious aspect. The decision to make baptism, rather than Confirmation, the qualification for lay people to appear on parochial electoral rolls was more inclusive than Anglo-Catholics wished; but although in law non-Anglicans retained many rights within their parish church, the sense that the Church of England was part of the nation rather than the whole was increasing. The rejection by Parliament of the proposed Prayer Book of 1928 had major repercussions for the relationship between the Church of England and the state. The introduction of synodical government in 1969 and the possibility of the Church of England legislating for itself in a number of matters by canon (including worship and doctrine after 1974), which did not involve Parliament, accentuated this sense of distinctiveness.

Early ecumenical developments

21 The Lambeth Conference of 1920 significantly changed the relationships between the Church of England and the Free Churches. The Wesleyan Methodist, John Scott Lidgett, noted the remarkable improvement in the atmosphere after 1920, even though the discussions between the Church of England and the Free Churches eventually broke down because of the insistence upon episcopal ordination for all Free Church ministers. It no longer seemed daring to join in common prayers and to exchange pulpits, and this became even more frequent after the Second World War and the formation of the British Council of Churches in 1942. In the 1940s and 1950s more ecumenically minded Anglo-Catholics were able to make common cause with 'Liberal Evangelicals', who shared an interest in liturgical revision concerned with bringing liturgy to life in contemporary language rather than restoring a primitive 'original'. A significant meeting of Anglican conservative evangelicals at Keele in 1967 led to a greater involvement by them in the new General Synod from 1970.

22 Some Wesleyan Methodists in 1918 had sought to keep a special relationship with the Church of England alive by opposing Methodist reunion, but this was short-lived. The main

ecumenical priority for Methodists in the 1920s was internal reunion. But, as the discussions over the Church of South India in the 1930s revealed, Methodism occupied a middle position between Anglicans and Congregationalists. After Archbishop Fisher appealed to the Free Churches to consider whether they could 'take episcopacy into their system' in his Cambridge sermon of 1946, the Methodist Church was the only one to respond positively; and this led to the Anglican-Methodist Conversations in the 1950s and 1960s.

23 By this time a number of things were changing. Among the Free Churches the rapid growth of the 19th century had given way to a gradual and then increasing decline. *The Free Churches and the State,* a Free Church Federal Council report of 1953, recognised that the 19th-century arguments about disestablishment needed review; and the House of Lords' decision in the Free Church of Scotland Case in 1904 had established that no church in Britain was free to change its polity and doctrine without the risk of losing its property, unless it sought parliamentary sanction. Thus the Methodist unions of 1907 and 1932 required accompanying parliamentary legislation, as did the United Reformed Church unions of 1972, 1981 and 2000. Other parliamentary legislation since 1951 has protected the position of various Free Churches in England, not least in securing that the decisions of their church councils enjoy some legal recognition.

24 The Second Vatican Council committed the Roman Catholic Church to ecumenism, and brought about a change in relations between Catholics and Protestants comparable to that which the Lambeth Conference of 1920 effected between the Church of England and the Free Churches. Thus the Roman Catholic Church became an observer in the discussions among the churches in England in the 1970s about the possibility of a Covenant for Unity.

25 The Areas of Ecumenical Experiment encouraged by the Nottingham Faith and Order Conference of 1964 have grown into the Local Ecumenical Partnerships (LEPs) of today. Although inter-church relations have become closer in some places than others, LEPs have broken down barriers and opened new possibilities for co-operation. This means that the churches are in a new situation today, even by comparison with the position 20 years ago when the English Covenant discussions broke down. Things unimaginable then have now happened. This creates a new openness to different perceptions of hitherto separate histories; it offers a new opportunity to discover and make visible the unity of the Church.

OUR CHURCHES TODAY

The Methodist Church

26 The Methodist Church in Great Britain believes it is part of 'the Holy, Catholic Church', called by God for mission and service. It is a community of just over a million people. Of these just under 300,000 are recorded as active members in England in more than 6,000 local churches. About the same number (300,000) worship in local Methodist churches each week. Local churches seek to exercise the whole ministry of Christ in a locality and to share in the wider ministry of the Church in the world. They are the primary focus for the ministry of worship Sunday by Sunday and for much of the church's wider outreach. They vary in size (with the numerical majority being small) and in the localities they serve, from city centres to small villages.

27 The geographical scope of the Methodist Church in Great Britain is England, Scotland, Wales, the Channel Islands, the Isle of Man, Gibraltar and Malta. Local churches are grouped into over 600 circuits within 33 districts. There are three districts in Wales, two in Scotland and one each in the Channel Islands and the Isle of Man; Gibraltar and Malta are each a circuit in a London district. In each district a minister is appointed as Chairman (or Chair) of the District (of the Methodist Synod in the case of Scotland); in all but four districts the chairmanship is a full-time post. The role of the Chairman is broadly defined as 'furthering the work of God in the District' and there is a specific responsibility of oversight and pastoral care towards ministers and leadership of all the people in the district. The Chairman is responsible to the Conference for the observance within the District of Methodist order and discipline.

28 Circuits are the primary units in which local churches express and experience their interconnexion in the Body of Christ for the purposes of mission, mutual encouragement and help. Ministers, deacons and probationers are appointed to the circuits and local preachers (see below) exercise their calling on a circuit basis. In every circuit there is one minister who is the Superintendent, responsible for upholding the discipline and decisions of the Methodist Conference, the governing body of the Methodist Church. He or she leads a team

that may include deacons and lay people exercising specific ministries (including administration) as well as ministers (presbyters). The Methodist Church has over recent years developed increasingly flexible patterns of ministry, both of the ordained and of the whole people of God. There are currently about 2,000 active ministers and over 100 deacons. There is a clear demand from circuits for more ministers than are currently available to be stationed; whilst the numbers entering training for ordained ministry have risen significantly, there is still an imbalance between those entering service and those retiring. Working alongside ordained ministries there are lay workers (paid and voluntary) and nearly 10,000 local preachers. The latter are lay people who are trained and accredited to lead worship and preach throughout the connexion. They conduct the majority of Sunday services in Methodist churches and almost all ministers have trained as local preachers before offering for ordained ministry.

29 The whole of British Methodism is currently engaged in a process, 'Our Calling', which focuses attention on four themes:
- Worship (The Church exists to increase awareness of God's presence and to celebrate God's love);
- Learning and caring (The Church exists to help people to grow and learn as Christians through mutual support and care);
- Service (The Church exists to be a good neighbour to people in need and to challenge injustice); and
- Evangelism (The Church exists to make more followers of Jesus Christ).

This process came out of a wide process of consultation and was endorsed by the Conference in 2000. It has been taken up with enthusiasm in many districts, circuits and local churches notably as a way of helping to shape plans and strategies for the future.

30 Methodism is active in work with children and young people. Local church activities are supported through an active connexional organisation (notably providing regular national youth gatherings and support for work amongst children). It also has some involvement in formal education as a provider of schools and colleges, often in partnership with others including (especially in relation to primary education) the Church of England. It has a strong commitment to critical engagement with government on education policy especially in relation to provision in the maintained sector of education.

31 Some areas of work such as partnership in world mission are core activities of the Church rather than being undertaken by voluntary societies as in some other traditions. In the same way work done in the area of child care by NCH and in the care of the elderly by Methodist Homes comes under the oversight of the Conference.

32 The Methodist Church in Great Britain plays its part, alongside 70 or so other churches with roots in the Wesleyan tradition, in 108 countries, in the World Methodist Council. These churches vary greatly in their polity and practice and the Council, which meets every five years, is consultative and co-operative rather than legislative. It has been the vehicle for international dialogues going back over 30 years with the Roman Catholic Church and, more recently, with Lutheran, Reformed and Anglican world bodies.

The Church of England

33 The Church of England comprises 44 dioceses (including the Diocese of Gibraltar in Europe and the Diocese of Sodor and Man), each one with its cathedral as the mother church of the diocese and the seat of the bishop. The dioceses are grouped into the two provinces of Canterbury and York, each with its archbishop. The dioceses are made up of parishes, each with its parish church and parish clergy. There are approximately 16,000 parish churches and chapels, 9,000 parochial stipendiary clergy, many thousands of non-stipendiary and active retired clergy, and some thousands of clergy in chaplaincies and sector ministries. Working with the clergy are 10,000 Readers and many Lay Pastoral Assistants and Evangelists (as well as Evangelists of the Church Army). Although the total number of stipendiary clergy is currently being eroded by the bulge in retirements, the number of ordinands entering training for both stipendiary and non-stipendiary ministry has been rising over the past few years and recognised forms of lay ministry have been burgeoning.

34 The Church of England is involved in working with children and young people, not only in Sunday Schools and church youth groups, but in statutory education at various levels. A quarter of primary schools are Church of England foundations and there are ten Church of England Colleges of Higher Education. The Church of England is currently seeking significantly to increase its involvement in secondary education. Many independent schools are Church foundations, as are most colleges of the ancient universities and this character is reflected in chapel worship and the ministry of a chaplain.

35 On a given Sunday nearly a million people attend Anglican places of worship. Given changing patterns of church attendance, it is thought that the total number of people for whom worship in an Anglican church is part of their way of life is several times that figure. It is estimated that something approaching half the population of England has been baptised in the Church of England. There is a large constituency of people who, though not regular churchgoers, remain within the Church of England's sphere of ministry in various ways. But there is also a substantial proportion of nominal Anglicans. Approximately 1,200,000 people are registered on Church Electoral Rolls for the purpose of taking part in church government at all levels.

36 The Church of England belongs to the Anglican Communion, a worldwide fellowship of 38 self-governing but interdependent churches that see themselves as at the same time Catholic and Reformed, episcopal and synodical. The Anglican Communion's instruments of unity and consultation are the 10-yearly Lambeth Conference of the bishops, the representative Anglican Consultative Council and the Primates' Meeting. The Archbishop of Canterbury has a special pastoral and presiding role within the Communion, but his formal jurisdiction outside the Church of England is limited.

THE HEALING OF MEMORIES

37 Methodists and Anglicans bring to the present stage of their journey together not only a common hope and vision of a united future, but also strong feelings that could continue to keep the two churches apart. These feelings, however caused, arise not only out of present unease but also out of past conflicts. They are fuelled by one-sided interpretations of their connected histories and exacerbated by the way that separated Christians easily slip into stereotyping. The stories, the historical memories become distorted.

38 Such feelings include disappointment, resentment, insecurity and incomprehension. It is vital that they be acknowledged in order that they may be overcome. Disappointed hopes over the failure of earlier unity proposals have also left painful memories and areas of anxiety that need to be allayed. The healing of memories is a necessary part of the healing of the wounds of division in the body of Christ.

39 Where our ministers and lay people work closely together, in leadership, local mission and theological conversations, these stereotypes are often broken down. We become aware of patterns of sympathy or lack of it that cross denominational boundaries. An agreement between our two churches would formally recognise the excellent relationships between Anglicans and Methodists in many spheres of activity and would itself help to promote the ecumenical healing of memories.

40 Our present divisions are not rooted in the formation of Christian doctrine at the early Councils. They are not Christological or Trinitarian. Nor do they reflect the progressive separation of East and West that came to a head in 1054 over the issue of universal primacy. Nor do they carry the freight of the major theological arguments of the 16th and 17th centuries between Roman Catholics and Protestants. Both of our traditions have been shaped by the Reformation. The extensive theological common ground between the Methodist Church and the Church of England is a striking feature of our relationship.

41 The reasons for the gradual separation of Methodists and Anglicans were complex and there were substantial doctrinal

differences, some recognised at the time and some noted subsequently. However, the genesis of our division lay more in pragmatic responses to circumstances than in doctrinal disagreements.

42 Anglican–Methodist separation may be seen as mutual estrangement which has changed both of us so that we cannot now think in terms of returning to where we were. Our culture as well as our theology and practice have developed independently and we will both need to move on if we are to find a new and common future. In this seeking of a new future, we need to bring our whole selves, past as well as present. That is why the careful discussion of theological common ground and of outstanding theological differences is vital. Our aim is not to put the clock back, to gloss over differences, and to construct a monochrome unity. It is to harvest our diversity, to share our treasures and to remedy our shortcomings, so that we may enjoy together what we believe God has already given our churches and still holds in store for us.

ANGLICANS AND METHODISTS WORKING TOGETHER

43 Methodist and Anglican leaders have worked together, along with leaders of other churches, for most of the past century in the ecumenical movement. There are now strong national and local relationships between Anglicans and Methodists in England.

In the ecumenical movement

44 The Church of England and the Methodist Church of Great Britain were founder members of the World Council of Churches (WCC) in 1948 and before that they played their part in the three strands that came together to form the WCC: Life and Work, Faith and Order and the International Missionary Council. They work together on the European scene through the Conference of European Churches (CEC).

45 Both churches were fully involved in the British Council of Churches, until it was dissolved in 1990, and take a leading role in the present ecumenical instruments, Churches Together in Britain and Ireland (CTBI) and Churches Together in England (CTE). Anglicans and Methodists are partners in 57 intermediate bodies (Churches Together in county and metropolitan areas) and in numerous groups of Churches Together locally.

In local unity

46 Grassroots ecumenism involving Methodists and Anglicans is particularly strong. They work side by side in local mission. They have committed themselves to local Covenants and other forms of Local Ecumenical Partnership (LEP). There are currently 861 LEPs of various kinds in England. Just over 500 of them involve the Church of England and the Methodist Church (in many cases together with other partners including the United Reformed Church). Of these, 198 are bilateral partnerships between Methodists and Anglicans (mainly single congregations in a shared building or congregations in a covenanted partnership). Such partnerships mainly involve local churches but there are also a significant number involving shared ministry to such areas as education, industry, local broadcasting, social responsibility and rural mission.

47 Local Ecumenical Partnerships, especially where they are a single congregation and share a building, anticipate in certain ways the goal of full visible unity that the churches nationally are still seeking to realise. They bring together into a common life diverse patterns of spirituality, worship and ministry. They live, worship and witness as one. To this extent, they challenge their parent churches to catch up.

48 On the other hand, LEPs highlight the fact that the churches are not yet in fact united. They do not have fully interchangeable ministers nor do they have a single focus of oversight and of decision-making. These two aspects are in tension and create some anomalies. Not the least of these anomalies are dual or multiple lines of oversight and authority, the fact that the churches are not able to own fully each other's ministers and the need to maintain separate membership rolls (reflecting somewhat different understandings of Christian initiation and of membership).

49 Many of those involved in LEPs long for the day when an agreement between the churches will gather up their pioneering work and rectify the anomalies that hamper local mission and fellowship. The realisation of that hope will only come with full visible unity at every level. But the new covenantal relationship made possible by the present proposed agreement will move us a significant step nearer to that goal. Eventually organic unity might supersede the arrangements for LEPs as far as Methodists and Anglicans are concerned. Meanwhile, many opportunities for growing together at every level of the lives of the two churches, together with encouraging examples of good practice, are set out in *Releasing Energy*, published by Church House Publishing and the Methodist Publishing House in 2000.

Collaboration in leadership

50 There is considerable consultation and co-operation between Anglican and Methodist church leaders at the national level. This has been enhanced in recent years. The two Archbishops and the President and Vice-President of Conference have an annual meeting at which they are joined by those with major national ecumenical responsibilities in the two churches. A fruitful meeting took place in January 2000 at Ampleforth Abbey between the Methodist Chairs of District and the Church of England's House of Bishops and a further meeting is planned for January 2002. Bishops and District Chairs already consult together in regional groupings and work together,

with the leaders of other churches, at intermediate level ecumenism in which various forms of shared oversight are exercised.

51 A series of regular meetings has begun between the Directors of the Archbishops' Council, together with senior ecumenical staff, and the senior connexional staff of the Methodist Church. There is a Methodist representative on the General Synod and a Church of England representative at the Methodist Conference. The General Secretary of the Anglican Council for Christian Unity attends the Methodist Faith and Order Committee and the Methodist Co-ordinating Secretary for Inter-church and Other Relationships attends meetings of the Council for Christian Unity.

Staff collaboration

52 There is also considerable co-operation and consultation between the central staffs of the two churches, in addition to that facilitated by the ecumenical instruments. Committees, panels and working parties tend to include a representative of the other church, who plays a full part in the work. In particular there is close liaison between the Church of England's Board for Social Responsibility and the Methodist Church and Society team. For example, the Methodist Church took the lead in the churches' response to the European Union Employment Directive in 2000 and in the preparation of material for use by the churches during the General Election campaign of 2001. In the field of education, there are a number of joint schools and a jointly funded Further Education Adviser's post. There is a good working relationship between those from both churches who are involved in the care of church buildings.

Shared ordination training

53 College-based ordination training is done in varying ways ecumenically in several places. In most (but not all) the Church of England and the Methodist Church are major participants. The Queen's Foundation at Birmingham is an integrated theological college, regional training course and research institute that is ecumenical by its constitution. The constitutions of some of the regional ordination courses provide a variety of arrangements in which the Methodist Church, and sometimes the United Reformed Church, are respected, though minority, partners alongside the Church of England. The validation and inspection of these courses is managed within an ecumenical framework, serviced by the Church of England, in which all the participating churches play a full part.

FIFTY YEARS OF ANGLICAN-METHODIST CONVERSATIONS

54 Anglicans and Methodists have long been committed to the quest for the re-union of the divided Christian Church. For Anglicans, a major milestone was the Appeal to All Christian People made by the 1920 Lambeth Conference. It presupposed that all the baptised were already united in Christ and proposed the Lambeth Quadrilateral of 1888 (the Holy Scriptures, the Apostles' and Nicene Creeds, the Sacraments of Baptism and the Lord's Supper, and the historic episcopate) as the basis for realising this unity in a visible way. (See also paragraph 18. The texts of the slightly different versions of the Quadrilateral adopted by the Lambeth Conferences of 1888 and 1920 are to be found in Appendix One.) The Appeal led to the first round of discussions between representatives of the Free Churches and of the Church of England.

An Anglican overture and a Methodist response

55 In 1946 the Archbishop of Canterbury, Dr Geoffrey Fisher, in a sermon at Cambridge, invited the Free Churches to consider taking episcopacy into their systems. This led to the multilateral report *Church Relations in England* (1950). The only church that formally responded to the invitation in these terms was the Methodist Church. Methodism has typically been open to unity overtures and has stated its willingness in principle to give up its separate identity as a church for the sake of unity. It has aspired to be organised for mission rather than for structural self-perpetuation and has seen unity as indissolubly linked with mission. These early explorations eventually led to the proposals for Anglican-Methodist unity in the late 1960s.

56 In these Anglican-Methodist proposals unity was understood to be not only spiritual, but also visible. Unity was already visibly expressed in the common confession of the apostolic faith and in a common baptism, but this was not sufficient to realise the inherent unity of Christ's Body. This required also a common ministry, one Eucharist and common structures of oversight and decision-making

as well. The model was that of organic unity, but not uniformity: a rich variety of church life would be served by a common order.

Towards a united church in England

57 The ultimate vision of the proposals that were widely debated in the late 1960s and early 1970s was of a re-united church in England in which the significant national mission of the Methodist Church and the national role of the established Church, eventually joined by others, would come together in a common witness and service. The goal was one church united for mission and service. The purpose of unity was mission. It was acknowledged that one of the causes of the decline in the influence and numerical strength of the churches was their disunity. Only a united church could effectively make the gospel known.

58 These talks were premised on a mutual recognition that they were between two churches within the one Body of Christ. It was accepted that each would need to be satisfied that the other maintained the apostolic faith and proclaimed the apostolic gospel. The doctrinal explorations were somewhat limited and presupposed the common ground on fundamental Christian doctrine, based on the Scriptures and the ecumenical Creeds, that had been already been established in preliminary multilateral discussions leading to the report *Church Relations in England*. There was a dissentient report by four of the Methodist representatives but the majority view was there were no insuperable doctrinal differences. It was felt that in a united church there was unlikely to be a wider range of theological views than in either of the churches separately.

Agreement on ministry and episcopacy

59 The talks of 40 years ago were able to formulate a common statement on Baptism and Holy Communion. With regard to the ordained ministry, they deployed the idea of a representative priesthood, as well as affirming the corporate priesthood of the Body of Christ. They concluded that the views of priesthood and ministry held by and within the Methodist Church fell within the limits set for Anglicans by their historic formularies. With regard to episcopacy, the talks accepted that the historic episcopate was not the only channel of sacramental grace and true doctrine, nor a guarantee of it. No particular interpretation of the historic episcopate was laid down. The reality of a corporately exercised *episkope* or pastoral oversight within the Methodist Church and centred in the Conference was acknowledged. The historic episcopate was seen as a 'sign and token

of the unity and continuity of the Church of Jesus Christ'. These positions became standard in the Anglican approach to ecumenical dialogue and were embedded in later agreements made by Anglicans with various ecumenical partners. They have been subsequently re-affirmed also by the Methodist Conference.

60 The talks envisaged unity being attained in two main stages. Stage one involved a reconciliation of churches and ministries, by means of a procedure that many found problematic, so that the ministry and sacraments of each church would be acceptable and available to the other. A Methodist episcopate would be consecrated to work in parallel with the Anglican episcopate. This stage was described, rather ambiguously, as 'full communion'. But it was acknowledged that this stage must entail a commitment to move on to the second, for 'the existence of two parallel Churches, side by side, in full communion, would be anomalous and unsatisfactory except as a step towards and a means of achieving the ultimate goal of union' (*Conversations Report*, 1963, p.9; cf. *Conversations Interim Statement*, 1958, pp.41ff). Stage two would bring about the complete union of the two churches.

The outcome of the unity proposals

61 Methodists and Anglicans prepared for unity by sharing in each other's worship and by taking part in local discussions. The Archbishop of Canterbury, Dr Michael Ramsey, gave strong support to the initiative. Though opposed by some Methodists, the scheme gained the required 75% support in the Methodist Conference. However, it failed to achieve a sufficient majority (also set at 75%) in the General Synod in 1972. This reverse was compounded by the failure in 1982, again in the General Synod, of the Covenanting for Unity proposals that also involved the United Reformed and Moravian Churches. After this it would be a long time before those Churches and the Church of England, for different reasons, would feel able to approach one another in the cause of unity at the national level and when they eventually did so it was on a cautious step-by-step basis.

62 In spite of these serious set-backs, there were some positive outcomes. In 1972 the Church of England extended eucharistic hospitality to baptised communicant members of other churches through Canon B15A (in line with the resolutions of the 1968 Lambeth Conference). Growing co-operation developed between Anglicans and Methodists (together with Christians of other churches) through what are now known as Local Ecumenical Partnerships and in local

Councils of Churches. The Church of England's ecumenical canons (B43 and B44), promulgated in 1989, provided a detailed basis on which Anglicans could participate in local unity arrangements.

A Methodist overture and an Anglican response

63 In 1994 the General Purposes Committee of the Methodist Church invited the Council for Christian Unity of the Church of England to join in preliminary talks 'to consider whether we share a common goal of visible unity and to identify the steps and stages required to realize it in the context of the wider ecumenical relationships in which both Churches share'. After consulting with the Standing Committee of the General Synod, the Council for Christian Unity responded positively to the invitation to set up informal conversations. These took place in 1995 and 1996.

International talks

64 Meanwhile, an Anglican-Methodist International Commission, the result of an initiative of the 1988 Lambeth Conference, had been meeting since 1993. Its report, *Sharing in the Apostolic Communion*, was published in 1996 and was welcomed by the World Methodist Council in 1996 and by the Lambeth Conference in 1998. The report found substantial accord between the two traditions in doctrine, sacraments and oversight. It believed that a future united ministry should be within the historic succession of episcopal ordination and invited Methodists to 'reclaim' this as a sign of the unity and continuity of the Church which Methodists had always affirmed and had provided for in other ways. The report concluded by recommending that the Lambeth Conference and the World Methodist Council should commend to the two world communions certain steps towards full visible unity. These are actually closely mirrored in the mandate of the Formal Conversations.

Commitment to Mission and Unity

65 The report of the informal conversations, *Commitment to Mission and Unity*, was published later in 1996. It affirmed that Methodists and Anglicans were in 'fundamental agreement' about the goal of visible unity and described this fairly substantially. It endorsed a method of moving towards this agreed goal by a series of steps or stages. It recommended the setting up by the two churches of Formal Conversations to implement this programme. The report sketched a number of possible ways forward and set the ecumenical

agenda firmly in the context of mission. It stated: 'We are aware that our separation damages the credibility of our witness in the world to the reconciling purposes of God. Moreover, it contradicts not only the Church's witness but also its very nature, and weakens our mission and evangelism in this country.'

66 *Commitment to Mission and Unity* also outlined an agenda for 'growth in fellowship' at all levels of the life of the two churches (paragraph 37(d)). This has been carried forward by an informal joint group and has resulted in the booklet *Releasing Energy* (see paragraph 49) which encourages various ways of expressing the developing relationship that can be undertaken by Methodists and Anglicans together.

67 Discussion in the two churches and consultation with ecumenical partners resulted overall in a fairly cautious welcome for the proposals of *Commitment to Mission and Unity*. This amber light was reflected in advice presented to the General Synod and the Methodist Conference in the report 'Towards a Response to *Commitment to Mission and Unity*' (GS 1266; cf. Methodist Conference Agenda 1998, pp. 80ff). Conference and Synod accepted the advice that Formal Conversations should be set up and that these should include ecumenical observers. They also agreed that trilateral informal conversations, involving the United Reformed Church, should run alongside the Formal Conversations.

THE FORMAL CONVERSATIONS

Their mandate

68 The mandate of the Formal Conversations is, therefore, a joint mandate of the Methodist Church of Great Britain and the Church of England. The Conversations were set the task of drawing up a Common Statement, on the model of the Meissen Common Statement between the Church of England and the Evangelical Church in Germany (EKD) of 1991. This model has also been followed by the Church of England in the Fetter Lane Common Statement (1996) with the Moravian Church and the Reuilly Common Statement (1999) with the French Lutheran and Reformed Churches (see Appendix Three). The common statement that the Formal Conversations were asked to work on was to comprise:

- A description of visible unity, based on the work of the informal conversations (*Commitment to Mission and Unity*, paragraphs 6-12).

- Within this description of visible unity, a section on what the two churches could agree in faith.

- An exploration of outstanding issues, especially those concerned with oversight. (It was considered that it was not realistic to carry forward into the mandate of the Formal Conversations all the issues mentioned in *Commitment to Mission and Unity*: some were deferred for further work between the two churches.)

- A Declaration in which the two churches would formally acknowledge one another as churches belonging to the one, holy, catholic and apostolic Church of Christ and would acknowledge the reality and authenticity of their ministries of word, sacrament and pastoral oversight.

- A formal Commitment to work together in all the ways that became possible at that stage (on the lines of *Commitment to Mission and Unity*, paragraph 37(d)) and to seek together, on the basis of the new relationship, to overcome any remaining obstacles to the fuller realisation of the visible unity of the two churches.

69 The overall purpose of the Formal Conversations is, therefore, that the two churches should take a significant step together on the way to the full visible unity of the Church. The agreements and Declaration, if approved, would bring about a new relationship of mutual acceptance, regard and commitment and so create a basis on which further steps to union can be considered. Mutual acknowledgement of the authenticity of the ministries of word, sacrament and pastoral oversight within the two churches should enable them to move from a situation of separate ministries to shared ministries, on the way to a single ministry.

How the Conversations worked

70 The Formal Conversations have been chaired by the Revd Dr John B. Taylor, former President of the Methodist Conference and currently Chairman of the Liverpool District, and the Right Revd Barry Rogerson, Bishop of Bristol and a President of Churches Together in Britain and Ireland. The Co-Secretaries have been the Revd Prebendary Dr Paul Avis, General Secretary of the Council for Christian Unity and the Revd Keith Reed, Assistant Secretary of the Methodist Conference. A number of participants from ecumenical partner churches played a full part. The full membership is given in Appendix Four.

71 The Formal Conversations have met nine times, seven of them being overnight meetings. Plenary and group discussion of prepared papers has been framed by worship and fellowship. All the members have been involved in preparatory work for this report. Informal work on the 37(d) Agenda, *Releasing Energy* (see paragraphs 66 and 68), has run alongside and there has been cross-fertilisation. The Conversations have given particular attention to recent ecclesiological statements of the two churches: the Methodist Conference Statement, *Called to Love and Praise*, and the report, *Episkope and Episcopacy*; and the House of Bishops' paper, *Bishops in Communion*.

The role of the United Reformed Church

72 The Trilateral Informal Conversations between the United Reformed Church, the Methodist Church and the Church of England reflect the close relationship of the three churches, not least the considerable number of LEPs where they work together. The

Trilateral Informal Conversations have taken place in conjunction with the Formal Conversations. There is considerable joint membership of the two sets of conversations. They agreed to operate a common pool of resources and a common circle of confidentiality. They have exchanged papers, at an appropriate stage of maturity, and have considered each other's comments on them. Thus the United Reformed Church has been able, to some extent, to follow, to monitor and to influence the progress of the Formal Conversations in two ways: through its two participants on those conversations and through its involvement in the Trilateral. Both sets of conversations believe that the response of the United Reformed Church to this report will be particularly significant and that the two churches should specifically invite such a response (see Recommendation 3, p.64).

The wider ecumenical context

73 We are also very aware that these conversations have implications for other ecumenical partners in these islands and further afield. We have been pleased to welcome, as observer-participants in the Formal Conversations, representatives of the Baptist Union of Great Britain, the Moravian Church in Britain and Ireland and the Catholic Bishops' Conference of England and Wales. We have been grateful for their specific input to our discussions. Their full involvement has continually kept us aware of the broader ecumenical stage. We acknowledge the importance of continuing to work towards appropriate forms of visible unity in partnership with the other members of CTBI and CTE. It is our further suggestion, therefore, that the representatives' meetings of these two instruments (the Church Representatives Meeting and the Enabling Group respectively) be invited to study and comment on our report (see Recommendation 2, p.64). The reactions of all our ecumenical partners will be important for further progress towards visible unity in Great Britain and Ireland and particularly for relations between Methodists and Anglicans in Wales, Scotland and Ireland.

74 Looking further afield, we look forward to receiving the comments of appropriate Faith and Order bodies within our world communions. It is our hope that the approach set out in this report, which follows closely that of *Sharing in the Apostolic Communion* (see paragraph 64) will be an encouragement and resource for Methodists and Anglicans to develop closer links everywhere.

SHARING IN GOD'S MISSION

75 Anglicans and Methodists share a conviction that unity and mission belong together. This is grounded in the indissoluble connection between mission and unity in Scripture – foundationally in John 17. In this key passage, both unity and mission are grounded in the truth of God's word as it is revealed definitively in Jesus Christ (John 17:6-8 and 17f.). As Methodists and Anglicans draw closer together in fellowship and increasingly collaborate in mission, they will want to seek together the truth of God revealed in Scripture.

Significant statements

76 Taking their cue from *Commitment to Mission and Unity (CMU)*, the Formal Conversations addressed their task by first laying a firm theological foundation for the connection between the two. *Commitment to Mission and Unity* suggests that the two churches share a common understanding of the Church's mission. In line with the faith and order tradition of the ecumenical movement since the International Missionary Conference at Edinburgh in 1910, that report links unity and mission closely together:

> The Gospel message . . . is compromised by our divisions, and consequently our witness to reconciliation is undermined. The Church is called to offer to the world through its own life the possibility of the unity and peace which God intends for the whole creation. The continuing divisions between our churches give an ambiguous message to a society which is itself divided in many ways.
>
> *(CMU paragraph 43.)*

77 The report goes on to comment that 'it is apparent that the lack of unity at the national level prevents local churches from realising their potential and from making their full contribution to the mission and catholicity of the Church.' Local ecumenical initiatives, it goes on, 'which are in the vanguard of witnessing to a reconciled and reconciling life', need the authority and support that would come from a national agreement (*CMU* paragraph 44).

78 The report of the Anglican-Methodist International Commission, *Sharing in the Apostolic Communion* (see paragraph 64 above), brings out the reciprocal connection between mission and unity. Unity empowers mission, while mission manifests unity and so reveals the true nature of the Church before the world (paragraph 37).

79 The recent Methodist Conference Statement on the Church, *Called to Love and Praise* (1999), also links mission and unity. They are bound to be 'closely related', it claims, 'since the Triune God who commissions the Church is One, seeking to reconcile and bring the world itself into a unity in Christ' (paragraph 3.2.1).

Koinonia and mission

80 God's plan is 'to gather up all things in him [Christ], things in heaven and things on earth' (Ephesians 1:9-10). God has made known in Christ the mystery of his eternal will and purpose. God's purpose is to draw redeemed humanity and the created order together into communion through Christ. Through his death and resurrection, he gathers into one the children of God who are scattered abroad (John 11:51-52). The unbreakable link between unity and mission derives from that fact.

81 The churches have come to use the New Testament language of *koinonia* (communion, fellowship, partnership, and sharing together in God's gifts) to evoke the new reality that God purposes to bring about in Christ. When two or more churches share more and more in local fellowship and mission and explore together theologically what they hold in common, they come to a conviction that the *koinonia* that they discern in the other church reflects the *koinonia* that they know within themselves. They thus discover a reality of grace in the Spirit that is greater than either of them and which embraces them both. They learn to see the Church of Jesus Christ in each other's churches and so to discern the authenticity (although incompleteness) of the ministries, sacraments and forms of oversight within them.

The Church in God's purpose

82 The Church is not incidental to but a central part of God's gracious purpose. Methodists and Anglicans have welcomed the ecumenical insight that sees the Church on earth as a sign, instrument and foretaste of the fulfilment of God's plan. The images

that the New Testament applies to the Church ('people of God', 'body of Christ', 'temple of the Holy Spirit', 'bride of Christ') suggest that the Church is called by grace to play a part in the fulfilling of God's purposes.

83 Thus the *koinonia* that we experience in the Christian community is not only a fellowship one with another, but also a relationship of communion with God that is both personal and communal. *Koinonia* stands for a full communion with God (2 Corinthians 13:13 (14), a sharing in the very life of God (1 John 1:3), a partaking of the divine nature (2 Peter 1:4). This means that the Church should never be defined merely in terms of its activities as an institution, but always in terms of the character and purpose that it receives from God through grace.

The mission of God and the Church's part in it

84 What can Anglicans and Methodists confess together about God's gracious purpose, the mission of God, in which we are called to share? That shared understanding will put our quest for unity into the right perspective and give direction to the ways in which it is worked out in practice.

85 Mission is grounded in God: it is always God's mission. Its content and unsurpassable expression is Jesus Christ himself. God purposed in Christ to reconcile the world to himself and was incarnate in Christ to bring this about (Colossians 1:20; 2 Corinthians 5:18).

86 By the power of the Holy Spirit, God graciously enables us, as unworthy but forgiven sinners, to participate in the mission of God. Because God's mission is definitively expressed in Christ, our participation is located in the Body of Christ, the Church. 'The Church's task is to participate in God's mission' (*Called to Love and Praise*, paragraph 3.2.12). In mission the Church seeks to reflect Jesus Christ in its life and worship and to proclaim him in word and deed.

87 The Church's work of mission is the Church's proper response to God's initiative of grace. Mission is properly the calling and task of the Church as such, living in communion and connexion. Mission is entrusted to the whole Church, not merely to a part of it. As the task of the whole Church, mission is the vocation and responsibility of all baptised believers, the *laos*, the redeemed and sanctified 'people of his own' (Titus 2:14; cf. 1 Peter 2:9), without distinction between ordained and lay Christians.

88 As an expression of the mission of God, the Church's gospel mission conveys God's saving power in its fullness and wholeness for the salvation or healing of humanity (cf. Titus 2:11). People are to be brought into a saving relationship with God through Christ, appropriated by faith. True mission considers humankind not as a collection of disembodied souls, but as embodied, social persons. Mission addresses the whole person, that is people in all their social, economic, political and cultural relationships.

89 Within that reality of human living and dying, loving and striving, suffering and rejoicing, God is already at work. We do not attempt to bring an absent Christ to an abandoned world. Mission is grounded on the theological conviction that Christ is already present to the world through the continual operation of the Holy Spirit. The mission of God to the world is constant and is not restricted to the Church (cf. John 3:16, 5:17). God is at work in communities, organisations and institutions that may have little or no overt connection with the Church, except through the Christian believers who serve and witness within them. God may also use these bodies for the advancement of the Kingdom. They may have something to teach the Church about what the Kingdom means, even though they may not explicitly acknowledge God's reign of justice and peace. The Church's witness is to the Christ who is at work in his universal mission and is known in his revealed gospel (Acts 1:8).

90 It is because the gospel of the redeeming love of God in Christ is embodied in Christian communities that mission is inescapably a matter that involves the Church. Mission is a dimension of the life of the Body of Christ, an expression of the nature of the Church. The *koinonia*, mutual participation in Christ, that Christians share is therefore essentially missiological. Mission is not something added on to the being of the Church but is the expression of its essential nature, the cutting edge of its daily life.

91 The Methodist tradition speaks of the life of the Church being sustained and structured 'on the way' by all the means of grace, the ordinances of the gospel. They include prayer, worship, Bible reading, hymnody and fellowship. But certain means of grace or ordinances are recognised as having a public, representative dimension. These are the ministry of the word and sacraments, the exercise of pastoral care and oversight, and forms of conciliarity (representative synodical structures for reflection, discernment and decision-making). In both our churches there are forms of public ministry which are recognised whereby some are given authority to carry them out on behalf of the whole body.

92 Because mission is essential to the Church's nature it follows that it must be related to the four dimensions of the Church that we confess in the Nicene Creed: unity, holiness, catholicity and apostolicity. Mission and unity once again prove to be inseparable. But it is not only the 'oneness' of the Church that shapes its mission. Its holiness means that it is 'set apart' by God's calling and election to serve God's purpose of righteousness and peace and must reflect those attributes of God in its own life. Its catholicity means that it aims to hold together the rich diversity of gifts and insights generated by the breadth of Christian response throughout many cultures. Diverse expressions of the gospel answer to the diversity of human needs and situations. Such diversity can therefore enhance mission. Finally, the Church's apostolicity means that it is sent into the world in intentional continuity with the mission of the Apostles, with their preaching of the apostolic gospel and teaching of the apostolic faith. All four dimensions of the Church – its unity, holiness, catholicity and apostolicity – require visible expression.

93 The Church is the redeemed community of the God who is Trinity. It is the creation of the purpose of the Father, through the work of the incarnate Son, by the power of the Holy Spirit. Its unity, evoked by the Spirit, bears witness to the unity between the Father and the Son. In this way, when the Church is united in the truth of Christ, revealed in Scripture, it draws people into the life of God (John 17:20-26).

Mission and unity focused in Christ

94 The drama of God's salvation to which Scripture testifies is focused in the person and work of Jesus Christ. He is the ground of our salvation and the model of our mission. The Church's work in mission and unity, indissolubly connected, should reflect the key themes in the unfolding story of God's saving activity in the world. Here, while not attempting to offer a full description of the person and work of Christ, we focus on aspects of Christ that illuminate our task, seeking to be faithful to the pattern that we find in him.

95 All of us are created in the image and likeness of God and in all of us that image is marred by sin. Through Christ's *incarnation* human nature is raised to a new dignity. Christ's incarnation also expresses God's commitment to human need and commits us, following Jesus of Nazareth, to a like compassion towards and solidarity with those who are oppressed and pushed to the margins of society. Incarnation commits us, in each time and in each place, to

engage with specific situations of need and not to offer merely a generalised response. Incarnation also implies that the unity of the Church must take visible and specific form. Unity is not something rarefied, abstract and invisible, but must be embodied. Unity proposals must make sense at the local as well as at the national level.

96 Christ's *cross* speaks of our forgiveness and reconciliation with God. It reminds us that forgiveness and reconciliation are fundamental human needs and that they are met by God's self-giving love. Before the cross, all are in the wrong, all may be put right with God. Before the cross, all are equal, all are welcome. And the cross provides a pattern for those whom Christ calls (Luke 9:23; cf. Matthew 16:23 and Mark 8:34): a pattern of self-emptying and of service, not of power-seeking and triumphalism. The cross is the paradigm of dying that others may have life (2 Corinthians 4:10-12; John 12:24). The cross shows us that the discovery of unity is costly and calls for a kind of dying. This is not optional, nor is it required of one party to a relationship and not of another.

97 Christ's *resurrection* means that God's ultimate triumph over all evil, suffering and imperfection is already anticipated and guaranteed. In Christ eternity has entered time, life has conquered death. Therefore the Church of Christ is called to a resurrection life in contra-distinction to the forces of death and despair around it. The power of Christ's risen life is at work within the Church and in the world to overcome the forces of alienation and division. That power fills his body and knits it together in one.

98 Christ's *ascension* speaks of his life taken up into God. It points to his present victorious reign and links his resurrection to his final coming (Acts 1:11). It reinforces our conviction of God's continued involvement in his Church and in the world around. But his reign is not confined to the Church: it affects the whole world order. The victorious Lord goes ahead of his Church in mission. The ascended Christ intercedes for the unity of his Church just as he did in his earthly ministry (Hebrews 7:25; John 17). The glimpses of the heavenly banquet that we now enjoy become a call to anticipate it in a common table.

99 Christ's *sending of the Spirit* at Pentecost means that the Church is no mere human institution or collection of men and women following unrealistic ideals of unity and service. The gift of the Spirit, received in worship, fellowship and prayer, empowers the Church for mission. The New Testament describes the Spirit as the Spirit of truth, of holiness, of life, of power, of love and of grace. The work of the Spirit is to shape the Church to reflect those qualities. Pentecost, when

the disciples were gathered together and spoke in tongues that could be understood, is the reversal of the confusion of languages at the destruction of the Tower of Babel (Genesis 11; Acts 2). The Spirit of Pentecost brings harmony out of discord, unity out of division. Within that divine concord, there is a rich diversity. The Spirit presides over an abundance of different gifts, different stories and different identities. Diversity is cherished; it is gathered together in unity. As well as the imperative to seek unity, the Spirit gives the freedom to explore diversity (Galatians 3:28; Ephesians 4:1-16). The paradox of unity and diversity finds its resolution in the life that the Spirit gives.

100 The *final coming or appearing of Christ's Kingdom* signals the fulfilment of God's loving purpose for his creation and the fulfilment of the longings of God's children. 'Your Kingdom come; your will be done!' The Church on earth embodies God's Kingdom only in imperfect and fragmentary ways. Christ is Lord of the Church and will judge it for its shortcomings. Yet it is called to be a sign, instrument and foretaste of the Reign of God. It is called to embody in tangible ways the cause of the Kingdom: justice and peace, freedom and love, reconciliation and hope. The Church's witness to that divine harmony is distorted when it is itself divided. As the report of the international Anglican-Reformed dialogue put it: 'The Church . . . contradicts its own nature and calling when its members are unable to live together in a reconciled fellowship' (*God's Reign and Our Unity*, paragraph 18).

FULL VISIBLE UNITY

101 The Formal Conversations were mandated by the Methodist Conference and the General Synod (cf. GS 1266, paragraph 30 (a); 1998 Methodist Conference Agenda, pp. 81ff) to draw up a description of full visible unity based on paragraphs 6-12 of *Commitment to Mission and Unity*, under the following headings:

A common profession of the one apostolic faith grounded in Holy Scripture and set forth in the historic Creeds.

102 The first component of full visible unity that is agreed in *Commitment to Mission and Unity* is a common profession of the one apostolic faith. This is the faith that is grounded in the Scriptures and set forth in the ecumenical Creeds.

Scripture and the Creeds

103 Both the Church of England and the Methodist Church ground their belief and teaching on the Holy Scriptures, which they hold to be inspired by God. They share the ecumenical Creeds. Both churches also have secondary, historic formularies. Both churches affirm the apostolic faith in their official formularies and celebrate it in their liturgies and hymnody. Indeed, the liturgical and doxological expression of the Christian faith is important to both traditions, stemming as they do from a common root in the reformed Church of England and beyond that in the medieval and patristic western Church. Both traditions recognise the principle *Lex orandi, lex credendi* (literally 'The rule of that which is to be prayed is the rule of that which is to be believed', a Latin tag that hints at the complex inter-relationship between the Church's worship and teaching).

Church of England formularies and other doctrinal statements

104 Canon A5 of the Church of England points to the Scriptures and under them to the 'Catholic Creeds' and other 'such teachings of the ancient Fathers and Councils of the Church as are agreeable to the . . . Scriptures'.

105 Authorised ministers, both ordained and lay, give assent to this 'inheritance of faith' as their inspiration and guidance under God 'in bringing the grace and truth of Christ to this generation' and making him known to those in their care. This is set out in the Preface to the Declaration of Assent (Canon C 15):

> The Church of England is part of the One, Holy, Catholic and Apostolic Church, worshipping the one true God, Father, Son and Holy Spirit. It professes the faith uniquely revealed in the Holy Scriptures and set forth in the catholic creeds, which faith the Church is called upon to proclaim afresh in each generation. Led by the Holy Spirit, it has borne witness to Christian truth in its historic formularies, the Thirty-nine Articles of Religion, *The Book of Common Prayer* and the Ordering of Bishops, Priests and Deacons.
>
> *(Common Worship* (2000), p.xi)

106 Subordinate to these authorities are various recent statements of a doctrinal nature that have been endorsed in various ways in the Church of England. There are three main sources of these. First, doctrinal statements are found in the ecumenical commitments entered into by the Church of England, such as the Meissen, Porvoo, Fetter Lane and Reuilly agreements. The second source consists of the teaching documents commended as theological resources by the House of Bishops, such as various reports of the Doctrine Commission (most recently We *Believe in God,* We *Believe in the Holy Spirit* and *The Mystery of Salvation*) and the reports prepared for the House by the Faith and Order Advisory Group (FOAG): *Apostolicity and Succession, May They All Be One, Bishops in Communion* and *The Eucharist: Sacrament of Unity (A Response . . . to One Bread One Body).* Third, there are two major ecumenical statements that have been acknowledged by the General Synod to be consonant with the faith of Anglicans: *Baptism, Eucharist and Ministry* (the Lima Statement, 1982), and the statements on Ministry and Eucharist contained in the *Final Report* of the Anglican-Roman Catholic International Commission (ARCIC) of 1982.

Methodist doctrinal standards

107 The doctrinal standards of the Methodist Church are set out in the Deed of Union of 1932. This states that Methodist doctrine is 'based upon the divine revelation recorded in the Holy Scriptures' and that this revelation is 'the supreme rule of faith and practice'. It also says that these evangelical doctrines are contained in John Wesley's *Notes on the New Testament* and in the first four volumes of his sermons. The Deed goes on to state that Methodism 'rejoices in the inheritance of the apostolic faith and loyally accepts the fundamental principles of the historic creeds and of the Protestant Reformation' (see Appendix Two).

108 In addition to the doctrinal clause of the Deed of Union, there are other statements of a doctrinal nature: the *Catechism* of 1986 and the reports on faith and order authorised by the Conference, notably the two volumes (in three parts) of *Statements and Reports of the Methodist Church on Faith and Order* from 1933 to 2000 (including *Called to Love and Praise*). The hymns of John and particularly of Charles Wesley have considerable significance in both shaping and expressing the faith of Methodists and are, of course, used very extensively by Anglicans and others. Those authorised for ministry in the Methodist Church give an assent to the doctrines to which the standards of that Church point.

Reason and experience

109 Both traditions recognise that it is the work of the Holy Spirit to bring the text of Scripture to life and to interpret it in the Church. Both traditions acknowledge that there is a range of views about the authority of Scripture and how it is to be interpreted today. Both give a place to reason, seen as God's gift to be exercised with humility and in deference to the mind of the Church, in discerning the message of Scripture for changed circumstances. The place of Christian experience in authenticating our appropriation of the faith is tacitly acknowledged in both traditions. The appeal to experience is a thread that runs through the spirituality of Anglicans as well as Methodists. An emphasis on the experiential assurance of salvation has been characteristic of Anglican and Methodist evangelicalism. However, neither Anglican nor Methodist official teaching gives either reason or experience a status on a par with Scripture as a source of doctrine.

A common confession of faith

110 A careful comparison of Anglican and Methodist formularies and of more recent doctrinal statements will show that the two churches stand side by side in confessing the fundamental apostolic faith as it has been received in the orthodox Christian tradition. This inheritance of faith essentially comprises the trinitarian and christological doctrines, ecclesiology, and the doctrines concerning salvation:

- the triune nature of God, Father, Son and Holy Spirit, who creates, sustains, redeems and sanctifies;
- the making of humankind in the image and likeness of God, the universal love of God for God's good creation, albeit marred by sin and suffering; and God's eternal purpose of salvation;
- the need of humankind to be saved from sin, alienation from God and eternal death.
- the incarnation of the eternal Word of God, in the person of Jesus of Nazareth who is truly human and truly divine – son of Mary and Son of God;
- the atoning death and resurrection of Jesus Christ in the fulfilment of God's saving purpose;
- the prevenient grace of the Holy Spirit at work in us;
- the justification of the penitent believer by unmerited grace through faith in Christ;
- the witness of the Holy Spirit in our hearts that we are children of God and heirs of eternal life;
- the power of the Spirit, working through the means of grace, to overcome habits of sin and to conform us more and more to the image of Christ and to bring forth in us the fruit of the Spirit;
- the apostolic faith regarding the Church, the ministry and the sacraments (see paragraphs 121-193).
- the final appearing of our Lord Jesus Christ, the judgement of the world by him, the eternal consequences of rejecting God's mercy offered in Christ, the final triumph of God's Kingdom of righteousness and love and the new creation.

111 Methodists and Anglicans do not necessarily confess the faith in the same idioms or with the emphases always in the same places. Moreover, there is diversity within each of the two churches as well as between them.

Two remaining tensions

112 There are two areas of doctrinal controversy where some theological tension remains, both between and within our two traditions.

113 The first concerns such questions as: whether human beings have freewill to respond to the gospel; whether divine grace is irresistible; whether Christ died for all or only for the elect; and whether those who are saved will persevere to the end. These particular issues were among those that historically divided Arminians and Calvinists. They continue to be very important for some Anglicans and Methodists. We do not underestimate the seriousness of these issues.

114 However, it is not the views of individuals, however influential, that need to be considered when churches seek to reach theological agreement with each other, but the official positions of the two churches as expressed in their formularies or doctrinal standards. In each of our churches these are susceptible to different interpretations. However, it is significant that they do not support either the doctrine of reprobation (predestination to perdition) or Pelagianism (the view that we can be saved through moral renovation in our own strength). They thus point to some common ground.

115 The Church of England's historic formularies, especially Article XVII, were certainly shaped by the Reformed theological tradition (as well as by Lutheranism), and teach the doctrine of God's electing grace. However, they are careful not to go beyond the patent sense of Scripture and they discourage speculation about the hidden purposes of God or the destiny of individuals.

116 The doctrinal clause of the Methodist Church's Deed of Union does not contain any explicit comment on this issue. It refers to the first four volumes of John Wesley's sermons and to his *Notes on the New Testament* which are clearly Arminian in emphasis. But it makes it clear that these secondary standards 'are not intended to impose a system of formal or speculative theology on Methodist preachers, but to set up standards of preaching and belief which should secure loyalty to the fundamental truths of the gospel of redemption and ensure the continued witness of the Church to the realities of the Christian experience of salvation'.

117 In practice, both churches permit a range of emphases, within the parameters laid down by the terms of assent, in the interpretation of Scripture. The way in which the terms of subscription to the formularies are expressed softens the impact of underlying historical controversies. We do not believe, therefore, that this issue, though an important one, should prevent closer unity between our churches, any more than it prevents communion within them.

118 The second area of tension concerns the doctrine of Christian perfection, a particular emphasis of John Wesley's teaching and of Charles Wesley's hymns. Once again, the doctrinal clause of the Deed of Union does not refer to this question, but Sermon XXXV of the Standard Sermons, the sermon on Christian Perfection, addresses it.

119 It is important to recognise the broad definition of 'perfection' employed by both Wesleys. It meant above all 'loving God with all our hearts and our neighbours as ourselves'. It is also important to recognise some variations or inconsistencies within John Wesley's teaching on this subject and the varied understandings of that teaching in Methodism since the Wesleys. The Methodist Church today includes a range of views on this topic. Methodist preachers are not bound to a particular interpretation.

120 These facts suggest that this issue also should not keep our churches apart. There is no limit to what the Holy Spirit can accomplish in the lives of those who are totally consecrated to Christ. Once again, without playing down the importance of this issue, we do not believe that it should prevent closer unity between our churches, any more than it prevents communion within them.

The sharing of one Baptism and the celebrating of one Eucharist

121 A vital dimension of full visible unity is the sharing of one baptism and the celebrating of one Eucharist. Anglicans and Methodists already recognise each other's baptisms and welcome each other's communicants to the Eucharist. This approach is grounded in theological agreement that goes back to our common roots and was affirmed in the unity discussions of the 1960s. It has been reinforced by the ecumenical convergence reflected in the Lima statement *Baptism, Eucharist and Ministry* (BEM) (1982).

Ecumenical convergence on baptism

122 The Church of England and the Methodist Church of Great Britain responded positively to the section of BEM that deals with baptism. This suggests that there are no significant differences of theological understanding between us as far as baptism is concerned. BEM's rich scriptural imagery of baptism is reflected in the liturgies of initiation of both churches. There is a range of views concerning the relation between water baptism, regeneration and the gift of the Spirit, but also a common recognition that these belong together. In our

churches baptism is generally seen as the essential first stage of a process of Christian initiation that includes Confirmation and participation in Communion.

123 As BEM affirms (B2ff), summarising Scripture, baptism is the gift of God and is administered in obedience to our Lord. Baptism is with water in the name of the Father, the Son and the Holy Spirit. It is the sacrament of our union with Christ in his death and resurrection. It signifies death to sin and newness of life in Christ. It is given for the forgiveness of sins. Baptism is the sign and seal of our common discipleship. Through baptism we are brought into union with Christ, with each other and with the Church of every time and place. Water baptism is linked in Scripture with the baptism in the Holy Spirit. BEM concludes that our one baptism into Christ therefore constitutes a call to the churches to overcome their divisions and to manifest more visibly their baptismal fellowship.

A common practice

124 Both our churches baptise infants and young children and will baptise adult candidates of any age. Both churches believe that the 'one baptism' of Ephesians 4:5 and the Nicene Creed means that baptism is unrepeatable and therefore they do not countenance 'rebaptism' (though both have a place for conditional baptism where there is uncertainty as to whether baptism has been previously or properly administered). The two churches were among those who gave formal approval to the Common Certificate of Baptism produced in 1972 by the British Council of Churches.

125 Each church encourages its people to present their children for baptism. However, both churches include loyal members who have hesitated to have their children baptised before they are able to profess the Christian faith for themselves. Anglican clergy are required not to refuse or delay baptism to infants (and indeed to adults), given suitable preparation of those concerned. Methodist ministers are required to baptise infants 'in appropriate circumstances'. Baptism by lay persons in a pastoral emergency is recognised in accordance with ancient tradition. Both churches face the challenge of ensuring the pastoral follow-up and ongoing commitment of those who undergo Christian initiation. Thus there is agreement between our churches on the theology and practice of baptism.

Confirmation

126 Both Anglicans and Methodists practise Confirmation, though there is considerable diversity in the theological understanding of Confirmation within each church. This diversity reflects the fact that, within the Christian tradition, Confirmation has been understood in a variety of overlapping ways. Fundamentally, however, as our liturgies show, Confirmation is regarded by both churches as a means of grace within the total process of Christian initiation. For both churches, Confirmation includes the re-affirmation of the baptismal promises by the candidate, accompanied by the prayer with the laying on of hands that God will strengthen the candidate in his or her discipleship through the work of the Holy Spirit.

127 In both churches those who administer Confirmation act on behalf of the universal Church in this act of Christian initiation. This is signified in two ways. In the Methodist Church local presbyters confirm by virtue of their ordination, while in the Church of England the bishop, the 'chief pastor' of the diocese, confirms. This means that recognition of Confirmation between our churches is not reciprocal. Anglican Confirmation is accepted by the Methodist Church. However, a confirmed Methodist would be required to be episcopally confirmed if he or she sought ordination or a licence (say as a Reader) in the Church of England.

128 As outlined above, there is basic agreement on the theology of Confirmation. The fundamental congruence of Anglican and Methodist understandings of Confirmation is evidenced in liturgies for joint Confirmation services, based on the rites of the churches concerned, and approved by the sponsoring bodies. There is also agreement that Confirmation requires proper authority and oversight. The difference between the two churches is confined to the identity of the minister: presbyter or bishop? The question of who administers Confirmation and how requires further discussion between our churches in the future.

Membership

129 Both churches use the word membership in various ways but both regard baptism as fundamental initiation into membership of the universal Church.

130 In Methodism those confirmed are immediately welcomed into membership of the Methodist Church, though Confirmation and reception into membership are distinct acts.

Methodist membership may also be conferred on those who are members of other Christian communions.

131 The Church of England approaches the question of membership on several levels, reflecting its traditional role in English society (see paragraph 20). All residents of a parish, who are qualified to vote in secular elections, together with those on the Church Electoral Roll who are not resident in the parish, may participate in the election of Churchwardens and all residents have certain rights in relation to baptism, marriage and funeral services. Any baptised resident can join the Church Electoral Roll and thereby declare himself or herself to be a member of the Church of England for that purpose, which can be held together with membership of another denomination. Regular worshippers who are not resident in the parish can also join the Church Electoral Roll, and it is those on the Electoral Roll who elect members of the PCC.

The Eucharist

132 As with baptism, so with the Eucharist; both churches responded positively to *Baptism, Eucharist and Ministry*. BEM affirmed (BEM E2-4) that in the eucharistic meal, in the eating and drinking of the bread and wine, instituted by the Lord, he grants communion *(koinonia)* with himself. God is acting in the mystery of the Eucharist, renewing the life of the Church, the body of Christ. In accordance with Christ's promises, each communicant receives assurance of the forgiveness of sins and the pledge of eternal life. The Eucharist eloquently proclaims the Lord's death until he comes. It is a great sacrifice of praise which, in anticipation of the ultimate redemption of creation (Romans 8:19-23), the Church offers on behalf of the whole creation. Christ unites the faithful with himself and, by virtue of his life, death and resurrection, includes their prayers within his own intercession.

Similar liturgies

133 Liturgical renewal has provided the most striking example of convergence between the churches, not least in the case of the Eucharist. Anglicans and Methodists attending recently authorised services of Holy Communion in each other's churches would be struck by the similarity of the structure of the rites. Both churches have become more eucharistically centred in recent decades, though non-eucharistic worship also flourishes in both churches. John Wesley held a high view of the Eucharist as a means of grace and exhorted his

followers to be 'constant' communicants. Charles Wesley's eucharistic hymns are a liturgical resource for Anglicans and many others.

134 The richness of meaning in the Eucharist has produced different theological emphases. These are mostly differences within rather than between our churches. Both traditions hold that Christ is present within the eucharistic action, through the operation of the Holy Spirit.

Differences of practice

135 There are, however, differences of practice with regard to the sacred elements. Anglicans are required by the Canons (supported by the Lambeth Quadrilateral) to use the fermented juice of the grape, whereas Methodists are required by standing order to use non-alcoholic wine. Methodists usually communicate in individual cups, while Anglicans regard the common cup as liturgically and theologically significant. The ancient practice, now common in Anglicanism, of mixing a little water with the wine, is virtually unknown in Methodism. Methodists might wish to question the symbolism of the prevalent Anglican use of individual wafers. Some Anglicans have come to appreciate the Methodist emphasis on the common dismissal of communicants. While both churches require that any surplus of the consecrated elements is to be disposed of reverently, Methodists do not insist that it is to be consumed.

136 Another difference in practice is that in the Methodist Church children who are baptised are encouraged to join in the sharing of the bread and the wine. After a period of varying practice the conviction has grown that children receiving communion best expresses the oneness of the whole baptised community sharing together in the Eucharist. Within the Church of England practice varies from diocese to diocese and parish to parish.

137 There is also an important difference with regard to eucharistic presidency, which will be discussed in the next section (see paragraphs 163-165).

138 Thus there is a variety of practice in the two churches with, in some matters, identifiable differences between our two churches. The Methodist Church is currently working on its understanding of Holy Communion. The Church of England has recently published the statement *The Eucharist: Sacrament of Unity*. It does not appear, however, that there are fundamental differences of understanding between us.

A common ministry of word and sacrament

139 Full visible unity certainly requires a common – that is to say, a united, single, integrated – ministry of word and sacrament. But, to be fully effective, word and sacrament need to be ministered in the context of pastoral oversight. Clergy and ministers are ordained to all three tasks, not just to the first two. Full visible unity therefore also requires a common ministry of pastoral oversight (for which ecumenical theology has employed the Greek word *episkope*, as used in 1 Timothy 3:1 and in some early Christian literature after the New Testament). That issue will be taken up under the next heading. It is significant that, on issues to do with ministry as well as baptism and Eucharist, both churches responded positively to *Baptism, Eucharist and Ministry*.

Understanding ministry

140 The Conversations have found it helpful to distinguish ministry, first from everyday Christian discipleship, vital though that is, and second from instances of Christian service that individuals may from time to time choose for themselves. The Conversations have come to understand ministry in a more specific sense, namely as work, undertaken in the service of the Kingdom of God, that is actually acknowledged, either formally or informally, by the Church. All baptised Christians may be called to such a ministry. All Christians have received a charism (spiritual gift) of the Holy Spirit through their Christian initiation. Every limb or organ of the body of Christ has a vital role to play for the well-being of the whole body (1 Corinthians 12). All may be called to minister in one way or another. As their ministry is acknowledged and owned by the community, they are seen to act in the name of Christ and his Church.

Principles of ministry

141 The Conversations have also been able to endorse several principles, current in ecumenical theology, that underlie the exercise of all Christian ministry.

142 All ministry is the ministry of Christ himself in his body the Church. He uses human agency to care for his people. Human agents will always be unworthy, but because it is Christ himself working through them, the efficacy of the means of grace ministered by them is unimpaired (cf. Article XXVI).

143 Baptism (in the context of full Christian initiation) lies at the root of all ministry. That is not to say that ministry is merely an expression of a baptismal mandate or that nothing is added to baptism in the commissioning of lay people and the ordination of clergy. But baptism underlies and grounds all ministry because it is through baptism (in the context of faith) that Christians are united with Christ in his death and resurrection and are incorporated into his threefold messianic identity as our great Prophet, Priest and King (1 Peter 2:4, 5, 9). Baptism incorporates Christians into the community that is called to witness and to serve.

144 Ministry is representative of Christ in his Church. Both Anglicans and Methodists respond positively to the idea of representative ministry. The logic of it is that Christ cannot be without his covenant people and his people cannot be without their Saviour and Lord. The public ministers of the Church represent Christ to his people. He makes himself present in blessing through the means of grace that he has instituted. Ministers represent him in the sense that he works through them and uses them. Ministers also represent the people of God in the ministry of word and sacrament and in public witness before the world, helping to articulate their faith, presiding at their worship and exercising pastoral oversight that is entrusted to the Church as a body.

Ordained ministry

145 With regard to the form of the ordained ministry, there are both common features and significant differences between our two churches.

The diaconate

146 In the Church of England, the diaconate is one of the three orders of ministry. Anglican deacons are ordained to a ministry of word, sacrament (though not eucharistic presidency) and pastoral care. Most but not all deacons go on to be ordained to the presbyterate after about a year. No-one can be ordained priest who has not previously been ordained deacon. The Methodist Church, on the other hand, has a distinctive, permanent diaconate which is at the same time both an order of ministry and a religious order with a rule of life. Methodist deacons are seen as a focus for the servant ministry of Christ and the Church. In the Methodist Church this is the intention in the ordination of deacons. They are not ordained to a ministry of word and sacrament. Candidates for the presbyterate do not undergo ordination to the diaconate first (see *The Methodist Diaconal Order* (1993) in *Statements and Reports of the Methodist Church on Faith and Order*, vol. 2).

147 However, there are distinctive deacons in the Church of England and more extensively within a number of other churches of the Anglican Communion. The current ASB Ordinal for the diaconate can support a distinctive diaconate. The report of the House of Bishops Working Party on a Renewed Diaconate *For Such a Time as This* looks at recent scholarly work on the New Testament concept of *diakonia* and at the emerging ecumenical consensus, as well as at the pastoral and teaching requirements of mission today. This initiative may give fresh impetus to the diaconate as a distinctive order of ministry. The Canons require that candidates for the priesthood should previously have been ordained deacon. There seems to be a need for further theological convergence on the diaconate.

The presbyterate

148 In ordination the intention of both our churches is to ordain to the presbyterate of the whole Church of Christ. In the Church of England, presbyters are commonly called priests, while in the Methodist Church they are usually known as ministers.

149 Both churches make use of the idea of representative ministry (see paragraph 144). This approach relates ordination both to the priesthood of Christ and to the priesthood of the body of baptised believers. The one without the other would separate Christ from his Body. This twofold representation can be demonstrated from the teaching of both churches.

150 The Methodist Church states that, 'as a perpetual reminder' of the calling of the whole people of God 'and as a means of being obedient to it, the Church sets apart men and women, specially called, in ordination. In their office the calling of the whole Church is focused and represented, and it is their responsibility as representative persons to lead the people to share with them in that calling. In this sense they are the sign of the presence and ministry of Christ in the Church, and through the Church to the world' (*Ordination* (1974) in *Statements and Reports of the Methodist Church on Faith and Order*, vol. 1, p.110). *Called to Love and Praise* points out that the New Testament directs us to 'the priesthood of the body of believers, rather than the priesthood of every believer'. The statement adds that, while the latter emphasis is not necessarily wrong, it is much more individualistic than the language of Scripture which stresses the interdependence and common life of Christians (4.5.1).

151 In the doctrinal clause of the Deed of Union the Methodist Church rejects the idea of a separate priestly caste, claiming exclusive priestly powers and mediating between the Christian and God. We do not believe that these strictures apply to the Church of England's doctrine of presbyteral ministry. It is well known that the word 'priest' is derived from the word 'presbyter'.

152 In the Church of England, the term priest is thought appropriate because those ordained to the presbyterate are related to the priesthood of Christ and to the priesthood of the whole Church in a particular way. The Reuilly Common Statement (between the British and Irish Anglican Churches and the French Lutheran and Reformed Churches) states:

> We believe that all members of the Church are called to participate in its apostolic mission. They are therefore given various ministries by the Holy Spirit. They are called to offer themselves as 'a living sacrifice' and to intercede for the Church and the salvation of the world. This is the corporate priesthood of the whole people of God (*Called to Witness and Service*, p. 28).

153 The Church of England also believes that there is a distinctive priestly ministry which is also derived from Christ himself and which is exercised by those ordained priest.

> The special ministry is ordained to speak and act in the name of the whole community. It is also ordained to speak and act in the name of Christ in relation to the community. Its authority and function are therefore not to be understood as simply delegated to it by the community. Consequently, in so far as its ministry is priestly, its priesthood is not simply derived from the priestliness of the whole community. Rather the common priesthood of the community and the special priesthood of the ordained ministry are both derived from the priesthood of Christ (*The Priesthood of the Ordained Ministry*, 1986, paragraph 142).

154 *The Priesthood of the Ordained Ministry* goes on to say that, 'in the exercise of their office', the ministry of bishops and presbyters is 'an appointed means through which Christ makes his priesthood present and effective to his people' (ibid.). The report then shows how the ordained priesthood relates to the common priesthood:

> The ministry of those who are called to the episcopate and presbyterate fulfils a particular service by strengthening and building up the royal household, the spiritual temple, the holy priesthood of all the faithful. They do this through their ministry of word and sacrament, through their prayers of intercession, and through their pastoral care for the community. Their ministry may be called priestly in that it is their vocation to help the whole people to realise their priestly character (ibid., paragraph 143).

155 The Anglican-Roman Catholic International Commission (ARCIC) agreement on ministry and ordination also relates the ordained priesthood to the universal priesthood of the baptised when it says of the ordained:

> Not only do they share through baptism in the priesthood of the people of God, but they are – particularly in presiding at the eucharist – representative of the whole Church in the fulfilment of its priestly vocation of self-offering to God as a living sacrifice (Rom 12:1). (ARCIC, *Final Report*, Ministry and Ordination, 13: p.36.)

156 The Church of England's understanding of ministerial priesthood is thus of a pastoral, preaching, teaching, and sacramental ministry. It cannot be separated from the role that presbyters and bishops have in presiding at the eucharistic liturgy (see *Eucharistic Presidency*). It is certainly not that rejected by Methodist standards. A priest in the Church of England is a person called and ordained to the same ministry of word and sacrament as is exercised by ministers in Methodism.

157 We believe that there is a common understanding of the presbyterate and that this provides a sound foundation for the eventual interchangeability of presbyteral ministries.

The episcopate

158 While in the Church of England it is bishops in synod who exercise a ministry of oversight in intentional continuity with the ministry of the Apostles, the Methodist Church exercises oversight, in intentional continuity with the ministry of the Apostles, through the Conference and through those ministers delegated by specific appointment to do so by the Conference. The Church of

England is a church ordered in the historic episcopate; the Methodist Church in Great Britain at present is not. In spite of this obvious difference, however, we believe that there is a significant convergence in both theology and practice. The 2000 Methodist Conference adopted the guidelines of the report *Episkope and Episcopacy*, including the statement (Guideline 4):

> In the furtherance of the search for the visible unity of Christ's Church, the Methodist Church would willingly receive the sign of episcopal succession on the understanding that ecumenical partners sharing this sign with the Methodist Church (a) acknowledge that the latter has been and is part of the one holy catholic and apostolic Church and (b) accept that different interpretations of the precise significance of the sign exist.

159 As we have studied recent theological statements of the two churches (*Apostolicity and Succession, Bishops in Communion, Called to Love and Praise, Episkope and Episcopacy, Commitment to Mission and Unity*), we have become convinced that there is substantial agreement in principle (see further below, paragraphs 167-176). Nevertheless, further work remains to be done.

Unresolved ministry issues

160 At this stage of the journey between our two churches, it is not necessary to agree on the precise means by which a common or united ministry might be achieved, though the Formal Conversations have given some attention to various factors that will have to be taken into account. Among these are the issues of whether the ministry of oversight should be open to women as well as men at every level and whether those not ordained to the presbyterate should be given permission to preside at the Eucharist. These two issues remain unresolved between our churches at the present time.

Women in leadership

161 'The Methodist Church unhesitatingly affirms its conviction that both the presbyteral and diaconal ministries are open to men and women' (*Called to Love and Praise*, p.47). The Methodist Church has had women presbyters since 1974. The Methodist Diaconal Order has been open to both men and women since 1990. (There had previously been a deaconess order to which only women were admitted.) All posts and positions within the Methodist Church that are open to men are also open to women. There are women

District Chairs and there have been women Presidents of Conference. The report to Conference 2000 on *Episkope and Episcopacy*, Guideline 6, made it clear that an episcopate in the Methodist Church would be open to women as well as to men. This principle is regarded as something that the Methodist Church has received from God and wishes to share with the wider Church. For many Methodists, any failure to recognise and accept the full ministry of women would constitute a serious theological obstacle to full visible unity.

162 The Church of England is currently engaged in an open process of 'reception', within an ecumenical context, of the rightness of the decision to open the presbyterate to women. It is collectively seeking to discern, in dialogue with ecumenical partners, whether the step it has taken is indeed the will of God for the Church. The Church of England also has put in place various arrangements to provide extended episcopal oversight for some of those opposed to women's priesthood on grounds of conscience. With the support of the General Synod, the House of Bishops has recently initiated further work on the theology of episcopacy and the question of the possible consecration of women as bishops in the future. There are, of course, a number of women bishops within both the Anglican Communion and the communion of Porvoo churches. The communion provided by these two sets of relationships is impaired by the fact that it is not possible at present for women bishops to exercise an episcopal ministry in the Church of England. Clergy ordained by women bishops elsewhere are not eligible to officiate as clergy in the Church of England.

Non-presbyteral presidency at the Eucharist

163 In the Methodist Church, where eucharistic deprivation would otherwise exist, named probationer ministers (who have not been ordained), lay persons (usually Local Preachers) and, on occasion, deacons (for whom this is not the ministry to which they were ordained) are authorised by the Conference, for a year at a time, to preside at the Eucharist. Decisions of Conference in 1994 and 1996 re-affirmed that lay presidency is permitted as a pastoral response in cases of deprivation.

164 The Church of England, on the other hand, restricts presidency at the Eucharist to those who have been ordained presbyter (or bishop). This principle has been re-affirmed in the House of Bishops' report *Eucharistic Presidency* on the grounds that the person who presides should be 'a sign and focus of the unity, holiness, catholicity and apostolicity of the Church, and the one who

has primary responsibility for ensuring that the Church's four marks are expressed, actualised, and made visible in the eucharistic celebration'. The report concludes that it is appropriate that 'the presidency over the community's celebration of the Eucharist belongs to those with overall pastoral oversight of the community, i.e. to those ordained as bishop or priest/presbyter' (*Eucharistic Presidency*, p. 49).

165 This difference of polity can cause tensions within LEPs (though Methodist partners do not usually ask the Conference to authorise non-presbyteral presidency at the Eucharist in LEPs that involve Anglicans). It would present a problem if the Methodist Church and the Church of England were otherwise ready to enter into organic unity (though the need for lay or diaconal presidency would be reduced by such a relationship). It is worth noting that some non-presbyteral presidency continues to exist within the communion of Porvoo churches.

166 In order to fulfil their specific task, the Formal Conversations are not required to resolve these two differences between our churches. They are not mandated to draw up a scheme for the interchangeability of ministries. For the present, it is sufficient to agree on the theological principles that must underlie a common ministry and to set down a few markers that indicate our belief that it can and should be achieved early in the future relationship between the churches.

Theological convergence

167 Both of our churches believe that they are a part of the one, holy, catholic and apostolic Church. In the Creed, they profess, as an article of faith, their belief in this Church. But they are clear that they are only part of the one Church and that the Church of Christ is made up of many particular churches. They share a sense of sorrow and penitence for the ways in which the unity of the Church has been broken over the centuries and remains fractured today.

168 The apostolic continuity of the Church is located in its faithfulness to the permanent characteristics of the Church of the apostles:

> witness to the apostolic faith, proclamation and fresh interpretation of the Gospel, celebration of baptism and the Eucharist, the transmission of ministerial responsibilities, communion in prayer, love, joy and suffering, service to the sick and the needy, unity among the local churches and

sharing the gifts which the Lord has given to each. (BEM, M34.)

169 These are features that are intrinsic to the *koinonia* without which a Christian body cannot be in any sense the Church. The life of the apostolic community of the Church – its worship, fellowship, teaching and mission – is necessarily served by an apostolic ministry. The apostolic community and the apostolic ministry go hand in hand. In the nature of the case, there cannot be an apostolic community without an apostolic ministry: the Church cannot be without the ministry of the word of God and of the sacraments. When a church recognises another church as a church belonging to the one, holy, catholic and apostolic Church of Christ, it thereby recognises the authentically apostolic nature of its ministry of word, sacrament and pastoral oversight (cf. the Meissen, Fetter Lane and Reuilly Common Statements, see Appendix Three). Any suggestion, therefore, that a common ministry could be created by one church bestowing on another something essential to a church, that it currently lacks, would not make sense.

170 Recent ecumenical agreements (Meissen, Fetter Lane, Reuilly – see Appendix Three) that the Church of England has entered into with churches that are not ordered in the historic episcopal succession are instructive for our situation. They demonstrate that the Church of England is able to recognise another church as a part of the one Church of Christ, participating in the apostolic mission of the whole people of God, and to acknowledge that in it the word of God is authentically preached and the sacraments of baptism and the Eucharist are duly administered (as Article XIX requires to identify a visible church) as a question distinct from the question of whether that church has a ministry within the historic episcopate.

171 These agreements demonstrate that the Church of England is able to acknowledge a non-episcopal church as a church belonging to the one, holy, catholic and apostolic Church. However, the fact that the agreements mentioned above are not agreements for full visible unity but bring about a stage on the way towards that goal, shows that the Church of England holds (as the Anglican Communion has held formally since the adoption of the Lambeth Quadrilateral in 1888) that ordained ministry within the historic episcopate belongs to the full visible unity of the Church. The reasons for this lie in the Anglican understanding of the episcopal office and its representative nature in focusing the *koinonia* of the Church in time and space. Anglicans must remain committed on this point, in discussions with non-episcopally ordered churches, if they are to be consistent with what they have said over many decades to the Roman Catholic, Orthodox and Old Catholic churches.

172 Both Methodists and Anglicans see ordination as an expression of pastoral oversight *(episkope)*. It is those who have oversight who have the authority to ordain. Both also are committed to exercising *episkope* in communal, collegial and personal ways (cf. *Commitment to Mission and Unity* 10(d); *Bishops in Communion*; BEM M26). In Anglicanism, that oversight is exercised in ordination by the bishop who thereby becomes a minister of transmitted authority for the ministry of word, sacrament and pastoral care. The conciliar (synodical) structures of the church provide the bishop with advice, support and training resources in making provision for an ordained ministry. This is an expression of the principle that bishops can only rightly exercise oversight with the agreement of the people of God. In the ordination of presbyters, other presbyters join with the bishop in the laying on of hands. In the Methodist Church, the oversight that ordains is exercised by the Conference through its corporate *episkope*. However, within the Conference, which is made up of representative lay people, deacons and presbyters, only presbyters (ministers) ordain and thereby become the ministers of transmitted authority for the ministry of word, sacrament and pastoral care. In both churches, however, lay people have an important liturgical role in ordinations: they give their consent to the candidate, pray that he or she may be given all needful gifts of grace, and affirm and welcome the newly ordained minister on behalf of the whole people of God.

173 Both Anglicans and Methodists are aware of the substantial ecumenical consensus that recognises that ministry within the historic episcopate should be a feature of united churches (as it already is of several in South Asia with whom Methodists and Anglicans are in communion). Methodists and Anglicans are mindful of the cause of unity with the Roman Catholic and Orthodox Churches and of the theological dialogues with those churches in which they are engaged.

174 The only issue of principle that divides the Methodist Church and the Church of England over the historic episcopate is the question of the ordination or consecration of women to the episcopate, as already noted. The Methodist Conference has affirmed on several occasions its willingness to adopt the sign of the historic episcopate as a step towards visible unity. The willingness of the Methodist Church to become a church ordered in the historic episcopate and thereby to

participate in the universal communion of episcopally ordered, reformed churches (and potentially beyond that as well) is of great significance for Anglicans. They see in this intention an endorsement by Methodists of an aspect of catholic, ecumenical ecclesiology that they hold dear. They are also given grounds for belief that, in due course, and after a process of transition, the common ministry for which both churches long will indeed be a reality.

175 The apostolic character of the ministry of a Christian church means that its intention is to provide a ministry in continuity with the ministry of the Apostles (see *Apostolicity and Succession*, pp. 29ff; *Called to Love and Praise*, p.20f). Both the Church of England and the Methodist Church ordain, as their ordinals testify, to the ministry of the Christian Church, not to a merely denominational office. In a state of regrettable separation, each church separately intends to provide what it believes to be an apostolic ministry of word and sacrament. This intended apostolic continuity is an expression, first, of trust in Christ's faithfulness to his Church, and, second, of the Church's obedience and faithfulness to the one apostolic mission. Both churches believe that God answers their prayers. Each believes this of the other. This is a further persuasive reason, if any were needed, why the process of integrating ministries cannot imply any deficiency peculiar to either church that would be thereby remedied.

Looking ahead in ministry

176 All the essential theological ingredients to bring about an integrated ministry in the future seem to be in place. Faith and vision are what are chiefly needed now. It should not be beyond the two churches, inspired by the Holy Spirit, to agree on the actual process of integration in the next steps, as they implement together the affirmations and commitments of the Covenant.

A common ministry of oversight (episkope)

177 The Church lives under the authority of Christ its Head (Colossians 1:18) and is led into all the truth by the Holy Spirit through the Word of God (John 16:13). In each generation it has to seek the mind of Christ (Philippians 2:5) and to be receptive to the guidance of the Spirit (Galatians 5:16, 25). The Church is a fellowship *(koinonia)* of those baptised into the royal priesthood of Jesus Christ. All baptised believers share in the threefold messianic office of Christ who is Prophet, Priest and King. Participating in his royal priesthood, Christians share in the governance of his Church.

Integrated oversight

178 The goal of full visible unity includes a pastoral oversight that is united and works as one in leading the Church in mission. Methodists and Anglicans are equally committed to this ultimate goal as they work towards closer unity themselves. Oversight is crucially of doctrine, sacraments and pastoral ministry. Our ecclesiologies are not compatible with separate, parallel structures of oversight between churches that were already united in doctrine, sacraments and pastoral ministry, except as a temporary anomaly on the way to full visible unity. The Report of the Anglican-Methodist Unity Commission of 1968 stated: 'The prospect of indefinitely continuing parallel episcopates appears an intolerable anomaly. It could not be right for the Methodist Church "to take episcopacy into its system" save on the basis of a firm resolve that the Anglican and Methodist episcopates should become one' (p. 8). The Methodist Conference in 2000 resolved: 'The Conference affirms its willingness in principle to receive the sign of episcopacy, on the basis of the Guidelines set out in the report, *Episkope and Episcopacy.*'

Patterns of oversight

179 As we have already seen, there are a number of informal expressions of joint oversight between our two churches, mainly taking the form of consultation rather than decision-making (for example, as well as the joint meetings of District Chairs and the House of Bishops, there have been joint sessions of District and Diocesan Synods). Formal joint oversight is also a feature of Local Ecumenical Partnerships. In many places, regional church leaders have entered into a personal covenant relationship. Such covenants represent a stage on the way to full ecumenical collegiality in oversight by creating a climate of ecumenical commitment, consultation and co-operation. In intermediate ecumenical bodies for the English counties, regions and metropolitan areas, District Chairmen and bishops share presidency with colleagues from other churches. The offices of Ecumenical Moderator of Milton Keynes and Ecumenical Dean of Telford are pioneering initiatives that involve Methodists, Anglicans and others. The joint publication *Releasing Energy* is stimulating local expressions of shared oversight.

180 The covenantal agreement between our two churches that these Formal Conversations propose, would justify formal arrangements for shared oversight, as a stage on the way to a single, unified *episkope*.

Communal, collegial and personal

181 Pastoral oversight in our two churches is exercised in communal, collegial and personal ways. Since this pattern was first proposed by the Faith and Order Commission report, *Baptism, Eucharist and Ministry* (M26) in 1982, it has become widely accepted. Both our churches have endorsed it in numerous ways (see, for example, *Episkope and Episcopacy, Bishops in Communion, Commitment to Mission and Unity* 10(d)). These three dimensions of oversight are all expressions of the vital organic life of the Church as a body infused by the power of the Holy Spirit, that is to say, of *koinonia*.

182 The *communal* exercise of oversight is an expression of the essential conciliarity of the Church. Conciliarity stands for the involvement of the whole body in the governance of the Church. Both our churches are governed by conciliar bodies at every level of their lives, both national and local. In conciliarity, the whole Church, lay and ordained, takes responsibility for its life and mission through representative structures. Through its conciliar structures, the whole body of the Church is enabled to listen, in all its parts, to the leading of the Holy Spirit and to seek the mind of Christ. Though it is the body of Christ, its human members struggle to discern the truth. In that struggle the Church may make wrong or imperfect decisions.

183 The *collegial* exercise of oversight is an expression of fellowship *(koinonia)* in oversight. It gives an authority beyond that of the individual in oversight. It stands for shared responsibility and the biblical precepts of partnership in the gospel (Philippians 1:5) and of bearing one another's burdens in order to fulfil the law of Christ (Galatians 6:2). It presupposes conciliarity, the communal form of oversight, complementing and upholding it.

184 The *personal* exercise of oversight gives a proper place to leadership in the Church and to the special gifts and callings of individuals. Both our churches seek to acknowledge and support gifts of leadership, nationally and locally. The personal dimension presupposes the collegial and the communal, complementing and upholding them.

Oversight in practice

185 The principles and practice of oversight in British Methodism are comprehensively set out in *Episkope and Episcopacy*, paragraphs 10-51. In British Methodism, *communal* oversight is exercised supremely by the Conference which is at the hub of the

Connexion. Conference oversees matters of faith and order and issues teaching documents and liturgies; it exercises discipline over church officers; it makes church law (subject to public law and the Methodist Church Acts); it has responsibility for the selection and training, ordination and deployment of deacons and ministers; it serves as a focus of unity. The Methodist Church Act 1976 gave Conference power to alter its doctrinal standards. In the case of significant changes in polity, the 33 districts (and sometimes the circuits and local churches) are consulted. But the final word rests with the Conference (cf. *Episkope and Episcopacy*: 12-13). The delegated oversight of District Synods, Circuit Meetings and Church Councils is also a *communal* expression of oversight. In all these councils the lay and the ordained share in exercising oversight.

186 Oversight is exercised *collegially* in various ways: for example, by the meetings of District Chairs, by the Connexional Team and by the Methodist Council. The Council exercises delegated oversight on behalf of the Conference and is charged with giving spiritual leadership between Conferences (*Episkope and Episcopacy*: 16). The Ministerial and Diaconal Sessions of Conference are examples of collegial oversight. In each of these sessions, members of the same order of ministry 'watch over' each other and take counsel together about the work of the Church, with particular regard to their own order (*Episkope and Episcopacy*: 25). The same principle is at work in ministerial sessions of the District Synods. In local pastoral committees oversight is exercised on matters to do with church membership.

187 'Personal *episkope* is widely exercised in Methodism' (*Episkope and Episcopacy*: 36). Oversight is exercised *personally* by ministers in local churches, Circuit Superintendents, District Chairs and by the President of the Conference as its representative. The office of all these persons 'is recognised as conferring authority and influence. They are respected as representative persons' (ibid.). 'It is important to the Methodist ethos that personal *episkope* should wherever possible be exercised in a collegial or a communal context' (ibid.: 37).

188 Oversight in the Church of England is exercised by the bishops in synod and by synods which include bishops. Bishops have special (but not exclusive) responsibility for doctrine, worship and ministry. Bishops are the chief pastors in their dioceses and are called to lead the church in mission. They are the principal ministers of word and sacrament in the communities that they care for. They provide for and oversee the ministry of word, sacrament

and pastoral care in all the parishes of the diocese. They share this ministry with parish priests in a collegial manner. Bishops normally have oversight of sector ministries within the diocese. They are responsible for the selection, training and licensing of ordained and accredited ministers. They have the ultimate responsibility for churches and churchyards. They administer the law of the church. The bishop presides in the diocesan synod, chairs the Bishop's Council and is *ex officio* chairman or a member of all statutory diocesan boards and committees. Bishops are called to serve the mission and unity of the Church.

189 In the Church of England as a whole, bishops exercise a collegial oversight (see *Bishops in Communion*). The House of Bishops forms one of the three houses of the General Synod, the others being the houses of Clergy and of Laity.

190 It is sometimes said that Anglican churches are synodically governed and episcopally led and there is some truth in this. But we need to remember that bishops are part of the governing synods and that other clergy and lay people (such as churchwardens and lay Chairs of synods) also exercise leadership. The General Synod makes church law through Canons and Measures (the latter being particularly appropriate for areas where the Synod is legislating for the first time; they need parliamentary approval). The Worship and Doctrine Measure of 1974 gave the General Synod certain powers to legislate in these two vital areas by Canon (i.e. without recourse to Parliament).

191 The Church of England's synods also play a crucial role in senior church appointments. The Crown Appointments Commission, made up of the archbishops, representatives of the General Synod and of the Diocesan Synod of the vacant see and the non-voting Secretaries for Appointments, proposes two names to the Crown through the Archbishop of the Province concerned (in a constitutional monarchy, the Sovereign acts on the formal advice of her ministers). The Prime Minister may ask for two more names before nominating one to the Queen. (Deans of cathedrals of ancient foundation are appointed directly by the Crown after consultation that includes the diocesan bishop.) A code of practice to guide the diocesan bishop in filling senior diocesan appointments includes consultation with members of the Diocesan Synod. The Formal Conversations were not asked to consider questions concerning the relation of church and state, but these important issues will need to be carried forward to future conversations.

192 In the diocese, the diocesan bishop has a personal oversight but exercises it in collegiality with his suffragans and archdeacons and communally in conjunction with the Diocesan Synod and the Bishop's Council (the Standing Committee of the Synod). Rural or Area Deans have a certain oversight on behalf of the bishop and work together with the Lay Chair of the Deanery Synod. In the parishes, the incumbent or priest in charge shares the bishop's personal oversight but is required to work collegially with the churchwardens and communally with the Parochial Church Council (as well as with other ordained and lay ministers). The two archbishops have a provincial personal oversight and are joint presidents of the General Synod. In a collegial mode they chair the meetings of the House of Bishops and the annual meeting of all serving bishops.

Getting the balance right

193 Though the distribution of authority is different – the Methodist Church having a more centralised system, in the Conference, than the Church of England with its 44 largely autonomous dioceses which are the primary units of oversight – the principles are common. Personal *episkope* in both churches is exercised in a collegial and communal context. Anglicans and Methodists are re-examining the balance between personal, collegial and communal expressions of oversight. For example, the Methodist Church is currently considering how personal oversight is exercised and whether that might change or develop and the Church of England is exploring what collaborative ministry involves at all levels of the Church's life.

AN ANGLICAN-METHODIST COVENANT

194 Having worked together on the various areas of agreement required by our mandate, we are now able to propose to our churches a new relationship in the form of a covenant.

AN ANGLICAN-METHODIST COVENANT

We, the Methodist Church of Great Britain and the Church of England, on the basis of our shared history, our full agreement in the apostolic faith, our shared theological understandings of the nature and mission of the Church and of its ministry and oversight, and our agreement on the goal of full visible unity, as set out in the previous sections of our Common Statement, hereby make the following Covenant in the form of interdependent Affirmations and Commitments. We do so both in a spirit of penitence for all that human sinfulness and narrowness of vision have contributed to our past divisions, believing that we have been impoverished through our separation and that our witness to the gospel has been weakened accordingly, and in a spirit of thanksgiving and joy for the convergence in faith and collaboration in mission that we have experienced in recent years.

AFFIRMATIONS

1. We affirm one another's churches as true churches belonging to the One, Holy, Catholic and Apostolic Church of Jesus Christ and as truly participating in the apostolic mission of the whole people of God.

2. We affirm that in both our churches the word of God is authentically preached, and the sacraments of Baptism and the Eucharist are duly administered and celebrated.

3. We affirm that both our churches confess in word and life the apostolic faith revealed in the Holy Scriptures and set forth in the ecumenical Creeds.

4. We affirm that one another's ordained and lay ministries are given by God as instruments of God's grace, to build up the people of God in faith, hope and love, for the ministry of word, sacrament and pastoral care and to share in God's mission in the world.

5. We affirm that one another's ordained ministries possess both the inward call of the Holy Spirit and Christ's commission given through the Church.

6. We affirm that both our churches embody the conciliar, connexional nature of the Church and that communal, collegial and personal oversight *(episkope)* is exercised within them in various forms.

7. We affirm that there already exists a basis for agreement on the principles of episcopal oversight as a visible sign and instrument of the communion of the Church in time and space.

COMMITMENTS

1. We commit ourselves, as a priority, to work to overcome the remaining obstacles to the organic unity of our two churches, on the way to the full visible unity of Christ's Church. In particular, we look forward to the time when the fuller visible unity of our churches makes possible a united, interchangeable ministry.

2. We commit ourselves to realise more deeply our common life and mission and to share the distinctive contributions of our traditions, taking steps to bring about closer collaboration in all areas of witness and service in our needy world.

3. We commit ourselves to continue to welcome each other's baptised members to participate in the fellowship, worship and mission of our churches.

4. We commit ourselves to encourage forms of eucharistic sharing, including eucharistic hospitality, in accordance with the rules of our respective churches.

5. We commit ourselves to listen to each other and to take account of each other's concerns, especially in areas that affect our relationship as churches.

6. We commit ourselves to continue to develop structures of joint or shared communal, collegial and personal oversight, including shared consultation and decision-making, on the way to a fully united ministry of oversight.

RECOMMENDATIONS

195 We make the following recommendations for the consideration of the governing bodies of our two churches.

RECOMMENDATIONS TO OUR CHURCHES

1. We recommend that this report (i.e. the Common Statement including the Covenant) be commended by the governing bodies of our two churches for study and response throughout our two churches, in terms to be mutually agreed, and that this process should include joint study where appropriate.

2. We recommend that the report be commended for study and comment to Methodists and Anglicans throughout the four nations, to all our ecumenical partners and to Churches Together in Britain and Ireland and Churches Together in England.

3. We recommend that, in the light of the Trilateral Informal Conversations that took place in conjunction with the Formal Conversations, the United Reformed Church be specifically invited to study and respond to the report and that its response be received by both our churches as part of a continuing three-way conversation.

4. We recommend that a small joint liaison group be established to progress and monitor the above developments until such time as the Joint Implementation Commission (see 6 below) begins its work.

5. We recommend that, following the process outlined in 1-3 above and subject to the support of the two churches at large, their governing bodies enter into the above Covenant on the basis of the understandings reached in the Common Statement.

6. We recommend that, subject to the making of the Covenant by the two churches, a Joint Implementation Commission be set up to carry forward the implementation of the above Commitments.

7. We recommend that the Joint Implementation Commission give priority in the next phase of our relationship to the question of the interchangeability of diaconal, presbyteral and episcopal ministries, on the basis of the theological agreement set out in the report.

BIBLIOGRAPHY OF PUBLICATIONS REFERRED TO IN THE REPORT

Anglican-Methodist Unity: Report of the Anglican-Methodist Unity Commission: 2 The Scheme, SPCK and Epworth Press, 1968.

Anglican-Moravian Conversations: The Fetter Lane Common Statement with Essays in Moravian and Anglican History, Council for Chrstian Unity, 1996.

Anglican-Reformed International Commission, *God's Reign and Our Unity*, SPCK and St Andrew Press, 1984.

Anglican-Roman Catholic International Commission, *The Final Report*, CTS/SPCK, 1982.

Apostolicity and Succession, House of Bishops Occasional Paper, Church House Publishing, 1994.

Baptism, Eucharist and Ministry [BEM], World Council of Churches, 1982.

Bishops in Communion: Collegiality in the Service of the Koinonia *of the Church*, House of Bishops Occasional Paper, Church House Publishing, 2000.

Called to Love and Praise: A Methodist Conference Statement on the Church, Methodist Publishing House, 1999.

Called to Witness and Service: The Reuilly Common Statement with Essays on Church, Eucharist and Ministry, Church House Publishing, 1999.

Catechism of the Methodist Church, Methodist Publishing House, 1986, updated 2000.

Church Relations in England, 1953.

Commitment to Mission and Unity: Report of the Informal Conversations between the Methodist Church and the Church of England, Church House Publishing and Methodist Publishing House, 1996.

Common Worship, Church House Publishing, 2000.

Conversations between the Church of England and the Methodist Church: An Interim Statement, 1958.

Conversations between the Church of England and the Methodist Church: A Report, Church Information Office and Epworth Press, 1963.

Conversations on the Way to Unity 1999-2001: The report of the informal conversations between the Church of England, the Methodist Church and the United Reformed Church, United Reformed Church, 2001.

Episkope and Episcopacy, in *Statements and Reports of the Methodist Church on Faith and Order 1933-2000*, volume 2, part 2, Methodist Publishing House, 2000.

Eucharistic Presidency: A Theological Statement by the House of Bishops of the General Synod, Church House Publishing, 1997.

For Such a Time As This: A Renewed Diaconate in the Church of England, Church House Publishing, 2001.

May They All Be One: A Response of the House of Bishops of the Church of England to Ut Unum Sint, House of Bishops Occasional Paper, Church House Publishing, 1997.

Releasing Energy, How Methodists and Anglicans Can Work Together, Church House Publishing and Methodist Publishing House, 2000.

Statements and Reports of the Methodist Church on Faith and Order 1933-2000, Volume One, 1933-1983, revised edition 2000; *Volume Two 1984-2000*, in two parts, Methodist Publishing House, 2000.

The Eucharist: Sacrament of Unity, Occasional Paper of the House of Bishops, Church House Publishing, 2001.

The Free Churches and the State, Free Church Federal Council, London, 1953.

The Meissen Agreement: Texts, Council for Christian Unity, 1992.

The Mystery of Salvation: A Report by the Doctrine Commission of the Church of England, Church House Publishing, 1995.

The Priesthood of the Ordained Ministry, Board of Mission and Unity, Church House Publishing, 1986.

Towards a Response to Commitment to Mission and Unity . . . *A Report by the Council for Christian Unity*, GS 1266, General Synod, 1997.

We Believe in God: A Report by the Doctrine Commission of the Church of England, Church House Publishing, 1987.

We Believe in the Holy Spirit: A Report by the Doctrine Commission of the Church of England, Church House Publishing, 1991.

Wesley, J., *Explanatory Notes upon the New Testament*, Epworth Press, Methodist Publishing House.

Wesley, J., *Wesley's Forty-Four Sermons*, Epworth Press, Methodist Publishing House.

APPENDICES

Appendix One: The Lambeth Quadrilateral

This is to be found in two forms, from the Lambeth conferences of 1888 and 1920:

1888 Resolution 11:

'That, in the opinion of this Conference, the following Articles supply a basis on which approach may be by God's blessing made towards Home Reunion:

- (A) The Holy Scriptures of the Old and New Testaments, as 'containing all things necessary to salvation', and as being the rule and ultimate standard of faith.
- (B) The Apostles' Creed, as the Baptismal Symbol; and the Nicene Creed, as the sufficient statement of the Christian faith.
- (C) The two Sacraments ordained by Christ Himself - Baptism and the Supper of the Lord - ministered with unfailing use of Christ's words of Institution, and of the elements ordained by Him.
- (D) The Historic Episcopate, locally adapted in the methods of its administration to the varying needs of the nations and people called of God into the Unity of His Church.'

As restated in 'An Appeal to All Christian People', adopted by resolution 9 of 1920:

'VI. We believe that the visible unity of the Church will be found to involve the whole-hearted acceptance of:

> The Holy Scriptures, as being the record of God's revelation of Himself to man, and as being the rule and ultimate standard of faith; and the Creed commonly called Nicene, as the sufficient statement of the Christian faith, and either it or the Apostles' Creed as the Baptismal confession of belief;

The divinely instituted sacraments of Baptism and the Holy Communion, as expressing for all the corporate life of the whole fellowship in and with Christ;

A ministry acknowledged by every part of the Church as possessing not only the inward call of the Spirit, but also the commission of Christ and the authority of the whole body.

VII. May we not reasonably claim that the Episcopate is the one means of providing such a ministry? . . .'

Appendix Two: The Deed of Union Doctrinal Clause

Clause Four of the Deed of Union, one of the foundational documents of the Methodist Church, reads as follows:

4 Doctrine. The doctrinal standards of the Methodist Church are as follows:

The Methodist Church claims and cherishes its place in the Holy Catholic Church which is the Body of Christ. It rejoices in the inheritance of the apostolic faith and loyally accepts the fundamental principles of the historic creeds and of the Protestant Reformation. It ever remembers that in the providence of God Methodism was raised up to spread scriptural holiness through the land by the proclamation of the evangelical faith and declares its unfaltering resolve to be true to its divinely appointed mission.

The doctrines of the evangelical faith which Methodism has held from the beginning and still holds are based upon the divine revelation recorded in the Holy Scriptures. The Methodist Church acknowledges this revelation as the supreme rule of faith and practice. These evangelical doctrines to which the preachers of the Methodist Church are pledged are contained in Wesley's Notes on the New Testament and the first four volumes of his sermons.

The Notes on the New Testament and the 44 Sermons are not intended to impose a system of formal or speculative theology on Methodist preachers, but to set up standards of preaching and belief which should secure loyalty to the fundamental truths of the gospel of redemption and ensure the continued witness of the Church to the realities of the Christian experience of salvation.

Christ's ministers in the church are stewards in the household of God and shepherds of his flock. Some are called and ordained to this sole occupation and have a principal and directing part in these great duties but they hold no priesthood differing in kind from that which is common to all the Lord's people and they have no exclusive title to the preaching of the gospel or the care of souls. These ministries are shared with them by others to whom also the Spirit divides his gifts severally as he wills.

It is the universal conviction of the Methodist people that the office of the Christian ministry depends upon the call of God who bestows the gifts of the Spirit the grace and the fruit which indicate those whom He has chosen.

Those whom the Methodist Church recognises as called of God and therefore receives into its ministry shall be ordained by the imposition of hands as expressive of the Church's recognition of the minister's personal call.

The Methodist Church holds the doctrine of the priesthood of all believers and consequently believes that no priesthood exists which belongs exclusively to a particular order or class of persons but in the exercise of its corporate life and worship special qualifications for the discharge of special duties are required and thus the principle of representative selection is recognised.

All Methodist preachers are examined tested and approved before they are authorised to minister in holy things. For the sake of church order and not because of any priestly virtue inherent in the office the ministers of the Methodist Church are set apart by ordination to the ministry of the word and sacraments.

The Methodist Church recognises two sacraments namely baptism and the Lord's Supper as of divine appointment and of perpetual obligation of which it is the privilege and duty of members of the Methodist Church to avail themselves.

Appendix Three: Meissen, Fetter Lane and Reuilly

In recent years, the Church of England has entered into several similar theological agreements with other Christian churches throughout Europe.

In the Meissen Agreement (1991) between the Church of England and the Evangelical Church in Germany, the two churches acknowledged one another as churches belonging to the one, holy, catholic and apostolic Church, with authentic ministries of word, sacrament and pastoral oversight. They also committed themselves to share a common life and witness and declared their intention to work together towards full visible unity.

Similar acknowledgements and commitments were made in the Fetter Lane Agreement (1996) between the Church of England and the Moravian Church in Great Britain and Ireland and in the Reuilly Common Statement (1999) between the British and Irish Anglican Churches and the French Lutheran and Reformed Churches.

Appendix Four: Participants

CHURCH OF ENGLAND PARTICIPANTS

The Right Revd Barry Rogerson, Bishop of Bristol (Co-Chairman)

The Right Revd Dr Peter Forster, Bishop of Chester

The Right Revd Andrew Burnham, Bishop of Ebbsfleet

The Revd Canon Bill Croft, Precentor of Peterborough Cathedral and Diocesan Director of Ordinands

Mrs Terry Garley, County Ecumenical Development Officer for Churches Together in Lancashire

Miss Vasantha Gnanadoss, Solicitor's Department of Metropolitan Police; Member of General Synod

The Revd Angus MacLeay, Rector of St Nicholas, Sevenoaks

The Revd Dr Judith Maltby, Chaplain and Fellow, Corpus Christ College, Oxford

The Revd Alison White, Durham Diocesan Director of Ordinands

The Revd Prebendary Dr Paul Avis, General Secretary of the Council for Christian Unity (Co-Secretary)

Dr Martin Davie, Theological Secretary of the Council for Christian Unity and Theological Consultant to the House of Bishops

METHODIST CHURCH PARTICIPANTS

The Revd Dr John B Taylor, Former President of the Methodist Conference; Chair, Liverpool District (Co-Chairman)

Mr Dudley Coates, Chair of the Board of Methodist Publishing House

The Revd K Hilary Cooke, Superintendent Minister, Bristol (Frome Valley) Circuit

The Revd Wesley Daniel, Superintendent Minister, London Mission (South Circuit)

The Revd Neil Dixon, Superintendent Minister, Leeds Mission Circuit, former secretary of the Methodist Faith and Order Committee

Dr Susan Hardman-Moore, Lecturer in Divinity, University of Edinburgh

Deacon Jane Middleton, Convenor, Committee for Local Ecumenical Development

The Revd Dr Neil G Richardson, Superintendent Minister, Leeds (North East) Circuit, formerly Principal, Wesley College, Bristol

The Revd Peter G Sulston, Co-ordinating Secretary for Inter Church and Other Relationships and Ecumenical Officer

The Revd Michael J Townsend, Chair of the Leeds District; Chair Faith and Order Committee

Dr Stephen Travis, Lecturer in New Testament and Vice Principal, St John's College, Nottingham

The Revd Keith Reed, Assistant Secretary of the Methodist Conference and former Ecumenical Officer (Co-Secretary)

ECUMENICAL PARTICIPANTS

The Revd Michael Bochenski, Baptist Union of Great Britain

Dr David Thompson, United Reformed Church

The Revd Sheila Maxey, United Reformed Church

Sr Dr Cecily Boulding OP, Roman Catholic Church

Mrs Jackie Morten, Moravian Church

INDEX

affirmations, mutual v, 1, 61
Anglican Communion 13, 50
Anglican Consultative Council 13
Anglican-Methodist Conversations
  9, 19-23
  and ministry and episcopacy 20-1
  overtures and responses 19-22
Anglican-Methodist International
  Commission 22, 28
Anglican-Methodist Unity Commission
  (1968) 55
Anglican-Roman Catholic International
  Commission, *Final Report* 35, 48
Anglican-Methodist Covenant v-vi, 1, 17,
  59-62
  Affirmations vi, 60
  Commitments 61
  recommendations 61-2
Anglo-Catholics 6-7, 8
Anti-State Church Association 7
apostolicity 20, 31, 51-2, 54
Apostolicity and Succession 49
Appeal to All Christian People 8, 9, 19,
  65-6
Archbishops' Council 18
Areas of Ecumenical Experiment 9
Arminianism 38
Asbury, Francis 5
ascension 32
assurance of salvation 36
Avis, Paul 25

Baptism
  and early unity discussions 19, 20, 65-6
  ecumenical convergence on 39-40, 41, 60
  of infants 40
  by lay person 40
  and ministry 45, 48
  as sign of unity 39
Baptism, Eucharist and Ministry (BEM) 35,
  39-40, 41, 44, 51-2, 56
Baptist Union of Great Britain 26
BEM *see Baptism, Eucharist and Ministry*
Benson, Edward White, Archbishop of
  Canterbury 7
Bible Christians 5, 6
bishops
  and Confirmation 41
  and District Chairs 17, 18, 55
  and ministry of women 50, 53
  and ordination 53
  and oversight 57-9
  see also House of Bishops; oversight
Bishops in Communion 25, 49, 53
Bishop's Council 58, 59

Board for Social Responsibility (Anglican)
  18
Book of Common Prayer 35
Bourne, Hugh 5
British Council of Churches 8, 16, 40
buildings, sharing of 17

Called to Love and Praise 25, 28, 29, 46, 49
Calvinism 4, 6, 38
Calvinistic Methodists 4
camp meetings 5
Canterbury, Archbishop of 13
Catechism (Methodist) 36
catholicism, and Church of England 6-7, 13
catholicity
  and episcopal succession 6, 49
  and unity 27, 31
Chairman of District 10, 50, 57
  and bishops 17, 18, 55
children
  admittance to communion 43
  work with 11, 12
Church
  as body of Christ v, 19-20, 29, 44, 56, 66
  and focus on Christ 31-3
  and the Holy Spirit 32-3, 36, 37
  and the Kingdom of God 33, 37
  membership of 17, 41-2
  and mission of God 29-31
  and purposes of God 28-9
Church Army 12
Church Assembly 8
Church of England 12-13
  in 18th century 1-2
  in 19th century 6-7
  and Calvinism 4, 6
  Canons 8, 21, 22, 34, 35, 43, 46, 58
  and Convocations 7-8
  and ecumenism 8-9
  and eucharistic presidency 50-1
  and Evangelicals 6
  high-church tradition 2, 6-7
  historic formularies 20, 34-5, 36, 38
  and Lutheranism 38
  membership of 42
  and Methodism 2-9
  and ministry of women 50
  as reformed 38
  and Wesley 2, 4-5
  worshippers 13
  see also bishops; doctrine; General
    Synod; government; oversight
Church of Ireland 7
Church Relations in England 19, 20
Church and Society 18

church and state 7, 20, 58
Church in Wales 7
Churches Together in Britain and Ireland 16, 26, 61
Churches Together in England 16, 26, 61
circuits 10-11, 57
class tickets 5
clergy
    Anglican 12
    Methodist *see* ministers
Clowes, William 5
Coke, Thomas 4-5
Commitment to Mission and Unity vi, 22-3, 24, 27, 34, 49, 53
commitment, mutual v, 1, 25
Common Certificate of Baptism 40
communion, 'full' 21
conciliarity vi, 30, 56
Conference *see* Methodist Conference
Conference of European Churches 16
Confirmation 41
Convocations of Canterbury and York 7-8
Council for Christian Unity 18, 22
Countess of Huntingdon's Connexion 4
Covenant, proposed v-vi, 1, 17, 59-62
Covenanting for Unity v, 9, 21
Covenants, local 16, 55
Creeds, ecumenical 19, 20, 31, 34-6, 60, 65
cross, and reconciliation 32
Crown Appointments Commission 58

deacons
    Anglican 45, 46
    Methodist 4, 12, 13, 45-6, 49, 50
    see also diaconate
Deed of Union (1932) 35-6, 38-9, 47, 66-7
diaconate 45-6, 49
diakonia 46
Diocesan Synods 55, 58, 59
dioceses 12, 59
Districts 10, 18, 50, 57
diversity
    in unity 31, 33
    within churches 37, 41, 43
doctrine
    Anglican statements of 34-5, 36
    and Formal Conversations 20, 22, 36
    Methodist standards 4, 35-6, 38-9, 46, 57, 66-7
    and Methodist-Anglican division 14-15
    remaining differences over 37-9
    sources of 20, 36

ecclesiology
    of Formal Conversations 28-9
    and Methodism 25, 28, 30
    and mission 29-31
ecumenism 12, 16-18
    and baptism 39-40
    early stages 8-9, 14, 65-6

ecumenism
    and healing of memories 14-15
    and intermediate bodies 16, 55
    local 15-16
education, involvement in 11, 12, 18
episcopate 7, 48-9
    and ordination 8, 22, 52
    as sign of unity 19, 20-1, 22-3, 53-4, 65-6
    and succession 6, 22, 48-9, 52
    and women 50, 53
    see also bishops; oversight
episkope see oversight
Episkope and Episcopacy 25, 49, 50, 55, 56
establishment 7, 9, 20, 58
Eucharist: Sacrament of Unity 43
Eucharist
    and admission of children 43
    and differences of practice 43
    and early discussions 19, 20
    eucharistic hospitality 21, 39, 61
    liturgies of 41
    presidency at 43, 45, 48, 49, 50-1
    as sign of unity 39, 60, 65-6
Eucharistic Presidency 50-1
Evangelical Alliance 7
Evangelical Church in Germany 24, 67-8
Evangelical Revival 1-2, 3-4
Evangelicalism, in Church of England 6, 8
Evangelists 12
experience, role of 36

faith, common profession of vi, 34, 35, 36-7, 51-2, 59-60
Faith and Order Advisory Group 35
Faith and Order Committee 18, 36
Faith and Order Conference, 1964 9
Fetter Lane Common Statement 24, 35, 52, 68
Fisher, Geoffrey, Archbishop of Canterbury 9, 19
For Such a Time as This 46
Formal Conversations v, 1, 22-3, 24-6
    and baptism 39-40, 41
    and the Church in God's purpose 28-9
    and Church membership 41-2
    and Confirmation 41
    and Eucharist 42-3, 50-1
    and *koinonia* 28, 29, 30, 42, 52
    mandate 24-5
    membership 25, 68-9
    and ministry 44-50
    and oversight vi, 24, 45, 48-9, 53, 55-9
    and significant statements 27-8
    and United Reformed Church 23, 25-6, 61-2
    and visible unity 34-62
    and wider ecumenical context 26
Free Churches, and ecumenism 8-9, 19
freewill, differences over 38

French Lutheran and Reformed Churches 24, 47, 68

General Baptists, New Connexion of 4
General Synod (Anglican) 8, 18, 35, 58
   and Formal Conversations 1, 23, 24, 34
   and unity proposals 21, 22
God's Reign and Our Unity 33
government
   in Church of England 6-7, 13, 53, 56, 58
   in Methodist Church *see* Methodist Conference
grace of God, differences over 38

Harris, Howell 4
holiness 4, 31, 66
'Holy Club' 3
Holy Spirit
   and baptism 39, 40
   and Christian perfection 39
   and the Church 29-30, 32-3, 36, 37
   and Confirmation 41
   and the Eucharist 43
   and ministry 60, 67
hospitality, eucharistic 21, 39, 61
House of Bishops 17, 35, 46, 50, 55, 58, 59

incarnation 29, 31-2, 37
infant baptism 40
initiation 17, 39, 41; *see also* baptism; Confirmation

Jesus Christ, as focus of mission and unity 31-3
Joint Implementation Commission 62
justification by grace through faith 37

Keble, John 6
Kingdom of God, and the Church 30, 33, 37
koinonia vi, 52, 54
   and Eucharist 42
   and mission 28, 29, 30
   and oversight 52, 56

laity
   and administration of baptism 40
   in Church of England 6-7, 12
   and Eucharistic presidency 50-1
   in Methodist Church 5, 6, 11
   and ordination 53
Lambeth Conferences 13
   1888 7, 19, 65
   1920 8, 9, 19, 65
   1968 21
   1988 22
   1998 22
Lambeth Quadrilateral (1888) 19, 43, 52, 65-6
Law, William, *Serious Call to a Devout and Holy Life* 3

Lay Pastoral Assistants 12
lay workers 11
leadership
   collaborative 17-18, 56, 59
   in Methodist Church 10
   see also oversight
Legal Hundred (Methodist Conference) 5
LEPs *see* Local Ecumenical Partnerships
Liberal Evangelicals 8
Lidgett, John Scott 8
Lima Statement 35, 39-40, 41, 44, 51-2, 56
liturgy
   Anglican 4, 5, 8
   of initiation 39, 41
   liturgical convergence 42-3
Local Ecumenical Partnerships (LEPs) 9, 16-17, 21, 25, 51, 55
Lutheranism, and Church of England 38

Manning, Henry 6
Meissen Common Statement 24, 35, 52, 67-8
membership of the Church 17, 41-2
memories, healing of 14-15
Methodist Church 10-11
   and Anglican liturgy 4, 5
   and annual conferences 4
   and Church of England 2-9
   divisions and reunion 5-6, 8-9
   and ecumenism 8-9, 12
   and episcopate 21, 55
   and eucharistic presidency 50-1
   growth 6
   membership of 10, 41-2, 57
   and ministry of women 49-50
   and nonconformity 2, 7
   see also doctrine; Methodist Conference; oversight; Wesley, John
Methodist Church Act 1976 57
Methodist Conference
   and Anglican representatives 18
   and discipline 10, 57
   as focus of unity 57
   and Formal Conversations 1, 23, 24, 34
   and lay members 6
   and Legal Hundred 5
   and oversight 5, 20, 48, 53, 55, 56-7, 59
   Presidents 50, 57
   and unity proposals 21, 22
Methodist Council 57
Methodist New Connexion 5, 6
Methodist Theological Institution 6
ministers (Methodist) 10-11, 36, 66-7
   and Confirmation 41
   probationer 10, 50
   see also presbyterate
ministry 44-50, 66
   and apostolicity 52
   as ministry of Christ 44, 60
   non-episcopal 7, 8, 52-3

ministry
  as representative 20, 45, 46, 48
  shared 16-17, 25, 52, 54
  united 21, 22, 44, 50, 61, 62
  unresolved issues 50-1
  see also clergy; diaconate; episcopate; ministers; presbyterate
mission
  apostolic 31, 52, 60
  and the diaconate 46
  as focused in Christ 31-3
  and *koinonia* 28, 29, 30
  local 16
  and role of the Church 29-31
  and unity v-vi, 1, 19-20, 22-3, 27-33
Moravian Church 4, 21, 24, 26, 68

New Connexion of General Baptists 4
Newman, John Henry 2, 6
non-jurors 3
nonconformity, and Methodism 2, 7

O'Bryan, William 5
ordinal, Anglican 35, 46
ordination
  episcopal 8, 22, 52-3
  in Methodism 6, 53, 54, 66-7
  by Wesley 4-5
  see also diaconate; episcopate; presbyterate
'Our Calling' 11
oversight
  in Anglicanism 22, 48, 51, 57-9
  as communal, collegial and personal 53, 55, 56-9, 60
  and Confirmation 41
  and Formal Conversations vi, 24, 45, 48-9, 53, 55-9
  in LEPs 17, 55
  in Methodism 4-5, 10, 20, 22, 30, 48, 53, 55, 56-7, 59
  and ordination 53
  shared 18, 55
  as sign of unity 20-1, 44, 49, 55, 60
  and Wesley 4-5
  by women 49-50
  see also bishops; episcopate
Oxford Movement 1-2, 6

Paley, William 2
parishes 12
Parliament
  and Church of England 7-8
  and Methodist Church 9
pastoral care 30, 45, 58
Pelagianism 38
perfection, Christian 39
Pietism 4
Porvoo Agreement 35, 50, 51

preachers
  itinerant 5, 6
  local 6, 10, 11, 50
preaching, open-air 4
presbyterate 4, 46-8, 49, 50, 53
  see also clergy; ministers
Presbyterian Church of Wales 4
priesthood
  of Christ 47-8, 54
  corporate 20, 46-8, 67
  representative 20, 45, 46, 48
  see also presbyterate
Priesthood of the Ordained Ministry 47-8
Primates' Meeting 13
Primitive Methodism 5, 6
Pusey, E. B. 6

Queen's College, Birmingham 18

Ramsey, Michael, Archbishop of Canterbury 21
Readers (Church of England) 12
reason, role of 36
reconciliation
  through Christ 29, 32
  Church as sign of v, 27, 28
Reed, Keith 25
Reformation, as common heritage 14, 36, 38, 66
regeneration, baptismal 39
Releasing Energy 17, 23, 25, 55
Representative Church Council 8
reprobation 38
resurrection 32
Reuilly Common Statement 24, 35, 47, 52, 68
revivalism, and Methodism 5
Rogerson, Barry, Bishop of Bristol 25
Roman Catholic Church
  Bishops' Conference of England and Wales 26
  and Church of England 6
  and ecumenism 9, 12
Rowland, Daniel 4

sacraments, ministry of 25, 30, 45, 48, 52, 57, 67
salvation vi, 36, 37
Scottish Episcopal Church 7
Scripture
  authority of 36
  and baptism 40
  and common profession of faith 34, 35, 60, 65
  and doctrine 20, 35, 36, 38, 66
  and mission and unity 27
Sharing in the Apostolic Communion 22, 26, 28
Simeon, Charles 6
Superintendant ministers 10, 57

73

Taylor, John B. 25
Thirty-nine Articles of Religion 35, 38, 52
training for ordination
   in Church of England 12
   in Methodist Church 11
   shared 18
Trilateral Informal Conversations 23, 25-6, 61-2
Trinity, common confession of 36-7

United Methodist Church 6
United Methodist Free Churches 6
United Reformed Church 16, 18, 21
   and trilateral conversations 23, 25-6, 61-2
unity
   and diversity 31, 33
   as focused in Christ 31-3
   and mission v-vi, 1, 19-20, 22-3, 27-33
unity, visible
   and common baptism 39, 65-6
   and common profession of faith 34, 59
   early proposals v, 14, 19-20, 65-6
   and episcopate 19, 20-1, 22-3, 52-4
   and Formal Conversations 22-3, 24-6, 32, 34-62
   and LEPs 17
   and ministry of women 50, 53
   and pastoral oversight 20-1, 44, 49, 55, 60

Wesley, Charles 3-4, 36, 39, 42-3
Wesley, John
   as Anglican 2, 4-5
   and Christian perfection 39
   and the Eucharist 42
   and Methodism 3-5
   Notes on the New Testament 4, 35, 38, 66
   and ordinations for America 4-5
   sermons 4, 36, 38-9, 66
Wesleyan Methodists 6, 8
Wesleyan Reform movement 6
Whitefield, George 3, 4
Wilberforce, Robert 6
women
   in Methodist ministry 49-50
   in ministry of oversight 49-50, 53
   as preachers 5
word, ministry of 25, 30, 45, 48, 52, 57, 67
World Council of Churches 16
World Methodist Council 12, 22

young people, work with 11, 12

An Anglican-Methodist Covenant: Study group material

This book translates key ideas from *An Anglican-Methodist Covenant*, to enable those from both traditions to begin to explore the implications together and with other partner churches in their local situation.

The material has been designed to allow small groups to study the ideas over six sessions with an optional concluding workshop. It can also be used as a basis for individual study.

Significant quotations from *An Anglican-Methodist Covenant* provide the context for a range of activities, discussion and suggestions for Bible study and prayer.

We are challenged to let God's mission shape Christ's Church.

Publication May 2002
ISBN 0 7151 5766 3
£3.95 (estimate)
Page count: 40 (estimate)

www.ingramcontent.com/pod-product-compliance
Lightning Source LLC
Chambersburg PA
CBHW051957290426
44110CB00015B/2274